What Jewish Looks Like
Text copyright © 2024 by Elizabeth Kleinrock and Caroline Kusin Pritchard
Illustrations copyright © 2024 by Iris Gottlieb
Illustrations of art deco pattern by mushan (pages viii-xi, 110, 112), apple by Marina Zlochin (page viii),
lulav and etrog by Elen Nika (page 32), film reel by Дмитрий (page 48), ship by BigJoy (page 67),
suitcase by gmm2000 (page 75), kitchen utensils by Ксениягромова (page 83),
hands by Buch&Bee (page 93), microphone by mitay20 (page 100),
cat ears by topvectors (page 108), telescope by Good Studio (page 108), stool and microphone by onetime (page 108),
White House by patrimonio designs (page 109), paint tube by panaceaart (page 109)

For information address HarperCollins Children's Books, a division of HarperCollins Publishers,
195 Broadway, New York, NY 10007.
www.harpercollinschildrens.com

Library of Congress Control Number: 2023948430
ISBN 978-0-06-328571-2

Typography by Jenna Stempel-Lobell

24 25 26 27 28 COS 10 9 8 7 6 5 4 3 2 1

First Edition

WHAT JEWISH LOOKS LIKE

WRITTEN BY Liz Kleinrock **AND** Caroline Kusin Pritchard

ILLUSTRATED BY Iris Gottlieb

HARPER

An Imprint of HarperCollinsPublishers

Table of Contents

Introduction

THE BOOK you are about to read is one that we wish had existed when we were growing up as Jewish kids across the country from one another. We hardly ever learned about Jewish heroes in books or movies, and when we did, they all tended to look the same: light skin, curly hair, nondisabled, and with ties to European ancestry. These folks were mainly cisgender, meaning they identified with the gender they were assigned at birth, and were in heterosexual relationships. While there are many Jews who fit this description, painting a singular image of Jews does not capture the community's expansiveness. Beyond this limited representation, Jews were often portrayed as victims rather than agents for change. However, we believe that no community should ever be defined only by the worst things that have been done to them by other people. Our hope in writing this book is to spotlight the diversity of Jewish peoplehood around the world, and to affirm and celebrate its beauty and power!

Some of the thirty-six leaders in this book you might recognize, and others' stories have existed only on the margins. Some lived hundreds of years ago and others are blazing trails today. While many have a connection to the United States, others are from places you may never have known were home to vibrant Jewish communities. This collection includes Paralympians and chefs, anthropologists and activists, dancers and dreamers. It features the first Deaf Academy Award winner and more than a few comedians. But while the individuals in these pages represent a range of identities, they are threaded together by one unmistakable truth: They're all Jewish people whose lives, work, and values have changed our world for the better.

In the long-standing tradition of Jewish curiosity, we hope this book introduces more questions than answers! These thirty-six remarkable lives are meant to be in conversation with one another and to high-light the nuance and complexity of Jewish identity. We've organized them not by career, but by their relentless commitment to core Jewish values. We've also integrated Jews in the Community highlights to showcase additional voices of fierce organizational leaders on the ground today. We hope this book sparks curiosity and leads you to ask your own questions. If you'd like to learn more, we encourage you to hit the local library and do some digging. And if you wish you'd seen certain other folks represented in these pages, build new lists and shout them from the rooftops! Most of all? We hope you see yourselves reflected in these pages, and that you feel not only inspired, but also affirmed.

Whether you are Jewish yourself or learning about Jews for the first time, by reading this book and sharing what you find, our legacy continues with you. So, what does Jewish look like to you? We can't wait to find out.

L'chaim!

MY NAME IS LIZ! If you close your eyes and picture someone Jewish, what does that person look like? Chances are that most people don't think about someone who looks like me. Growing up Korean American, Jewish, and queer, I was the only person who looked like me at synagogue, Hebrew school, and Jewish summer camp. Jews, non-Jews, kids, and adults (even rabbis) would tell me, "You don't look Jewish!" Because of these experiences, I often felt like I didn't belong and that I always had to "prove" my Jewishness.

Now I'm an adult, and I've realized I don't want to spend my energy trying to convince people that I belong to the Jewish community. Instead, I want to expand people's understanding of Jewish identity and history, and help people realize that Jews who look like me and beyond exist and have always existed.

—LIZ

HI, I'M CAROLINE! I'll never forget the first time my grandpa shared the expression "two Jews, three opinions." I remember feeling an immediate, spine-tingling sense of connection. It reminded me that my pull toward exploring and questioning were all intrinsically tied to my Jewishness. It didn't matter that I often felt different from my peers while growing up in Texas—the holidays my family did (and didn't) celebrate, the food we ate, our extra Hebrew schooling . . . even our sense of humor! I knew in my bones that I belonged.

It wasn't until much later in life that I came to understand not all Jewish kids shared this same sense of belonging. I took for granted the gift of having my own identity reflected back to me in Jewish spaces, which means I've also played a role in upholding harmful stereotypes. I now understand "two Jews, three opinions" to mean more than just our collective pull toward a lively debate. To me, it celebrates how there are countless ways to be Jewish, and that each is not just valid, but beautiful.

—CAROLINE

Big Questions

How many Jewish people are in the world?

There are approximately fifteen million Jewish people in the world. That is only 2 percent of the US population and 0.2 percent of the world's population!

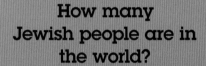

What is an ethnoreligion?

Jewish people existed long before certain categories like religion or even the term *Jew* ever came to be. The word *Jew* was derived from the word *Yehudi*, which means "from the Kingdom of Judah," the biblical Southern Kingdom. Today, Judaism is often described as an ethnoreligion. This term encompasses **a group of people who share a common religion and ethnic background**, which captures key features of Jewish peoplehood. Religion is an organized set of beliefs and practices that often connect to worshiping a higher power. Judaism is a monotheistic religion that draws from the Hebrew Bible, rabbinical wisdom, and other sources. Meanwhile, ethnicity is based on shared culture and background. While there is now a range of Jewish ethnic subgroups located around the world, Jewish people are known as a tribe and nation that share an ancestry beginning thousands of years ago in ancient Canaan (modern-day Israel, Palestine, Syria, Lebanon, and Jordan). Through the years, Jews have also been referred to as Hebrews and Israelites.

Are Jews a race?

Some people believe that Jews are a racial group, but this is false. Race is a social construct, which means people invented the idea of race as a way of classifying, labeling, and even demeaning others based on physical characteristics like skin color, hair texture, and more. **Jews do not come from one single racial identity, but instead represent a range of racial backgrounds and identities.** Portraying Jews as a race is a harmful practice that has been used to persecute Jewish people around the world for centuries. From the scapegoating of Jews during the bubonic plague in Europe and the colonization of areas of Western Asia and North Africa to the most famous example of Nazis targeting Jews as a racial group as a justification for genocide during the Holocaust, labeling Jews as a separate race has been used to rationalize exclusion and violence. However, throughout history, there have been Jewish people of every race around the world. Jews are a multiracial and multiethnic community.

Are Jews White?

In mainstream media and culture, Jews are often portrayed as White with European ancestry. Ashkenazi Jews are one ethnic subgroup with family who lived in Europe for generations. But **there are Jews of color living all around the world**, including Ashkenazi Jews! When people label all Jews as White and European, they erase both our ancestral origins and Jewish people of color.

The racialization of Jews has also changed in the past generation. In the United States, Jews were historically denied jobs, immigration, housing, and other rights based on the antisemitic belief that they were an inferior race. Because of this, Jews were not considered or accepted as White. Today, due to assimilation and present-day understandings of race, some Jews consider themselves White and some identify as White-passing or White-presenting. (Remember, race is a social construct!)

What is antisemitism?

Let's be clear: Jews haven't been discriminated against because there is anything wrong with being Jewish. Jews have been and are still discriminated against because of antisemitism and White supremacy. While antisemitism predates the concept of White supremacy, it has become one of its core pillars.

Antisemitism is one of the oldest forms of hatred, and there are many examples of it spanning back thousands of years. At its core, **antisemitism includes hatred of Jews, discrimination toward Jews, and negative beliefs about Jews**.

It takes on many forms and exists in every community, regardless of political beliefs or other markers of identity. Some of the most common forms of antisemitism are conspiracy theories that perpetuate the idea that Jews are a small minority who secretly control parts of society, such as politics, the media, or even the weather. Another key form is scapegoating, which involves blaming Jews for unrelated problems and issues around the world. These harmful beliefs often result in Jewish people being treated unfairly by others, being blamed for events they have no connection to, and being physically attacked, as well as synagogues being defaced.

*Note: The term *semitic* refers to a family of Afroasiatic languages that include Hebrew, Aramaic, and Arabic, and some people think that if they speak one of these languages, they can't be antisemitic. However, the term *antisemitic* specifically refers to hostility toward Jewish people, not discrimination based on the language you speak. This is also why there is no hyphen in antisemitism.

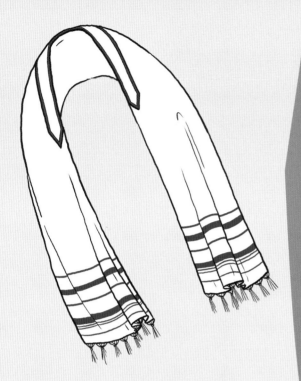

Do all Jewish people practice Judaism the same way?

People are Jewish either through their family lineage or through a formal conversion process. There are different Jewish denominations, such as Orthodox, Conservative, Reform, and Reconstructionist. Different movements have different types of observances and interpret religious laws in different ways. While Jewish people share many things in common, there still are many differences in how they identify and do (or don't!) practice Judaism. Jewish observance, spirituality, and cultural connections are a spectrum. **There is no one way to be Jewish!**

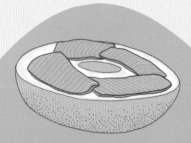

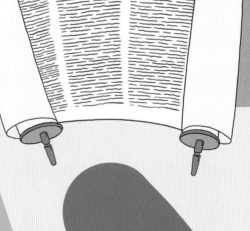

What is the Jewish diaspora?

"Where are you from?" This might seem like a simple question, but it can be difficult and sometimes painful for Jews to answer it. Today, the majority of Jewish people around the world belong to the Jewish diaspora, which is **the dispersion of the Jewish people from their original homeland** in present-day Israel and Palestine. In fact, one of the root functions of the word *diaspora* was to specifically describe the scattering of Jewish people after the fall of Jerusalem in the sixth century BCE.

Map

Jews dispersed across the globe as a result of antisemitism and colonization, but they found a way to thrive! Like many communities, Jews also migrated to pursue opportunity. Their communities remained largely insulated from the rest of the population, often due to rules dictating who Jews could marry, where they could live, and the jobs they could work. Despite these boundaries, they also integrated the customs and languages from their new homes to birth a diversity of Jewish traditions. The labels and categories included here are expansive, yet have their limitations due to the overlap and complexity of Jewish communities around the world.

ASHKENAZI

Ashkenazi Jews can trace their lineage through ancestors who settled along the Rhine River and spread across Eastern and Central Europe. Much of American mainstream Jewish culture, like matzah balls, kugel, and the Yiddish language, hails from Ashkenazi roots.

SEPHARDIC

Sephardic Jews migrated to and were later expelled from the Iberian Peninsula, which includes Spain and Portugal. They fled to Turkey, Italy, Greece, parts of North Africa, and other locations across Europe and the Arab World, even to Latin America and the Caribbean. They developed their own rich language called Ladino, or Judeo-Spanish.

LATIN AMERICAN

Jews were violently persecuted and expelled from Spain prior to and throughout the Spanish Inquisition. Some Jews fled to what would become Latin America. Even though many were forced to convert to Catholicism, some became known as crypto-Jews, or *conversos*. These Jews pretended to be Catholic as a means of survival but continued practicing Judaism in secret. During and after the Holocaust, many Ashkenazi Jews migrated to Latin America for safety.

MIZRAHI

In Hebrew, *Mizrahi* means "Eastern." The term had been used to describe Jews who remained in the Levant and migrated through the Middle East or Western and Central Asia and North Africa. Some of the largest and oldest Mizrahi communities lived in modern-day Yemen, Iraq, and Iran, including Bukharan Jews. While "Mizrahi" has often been used as a catch-all for Jews who did not fit under the "Ashkenazi" category, and often as a way to other them, today this term has been reclaimed by many in the community.

ASIAN

Many Jewish communities formed across Asia through the diaspora. The Cochin Jewish community was the largest and oldest in India and dates back thousands of years. Other Asian Jewish communities include the Kaifeng Jews of China and the Tamil Thattar Jews of Sri Lanka.

AFRICAN

Jewish communities in Africa have a rich and lengthy history. According to oral tradition, the Lemba Jews of Zimbabwe are descended from those who left the land of Israel over two thousand years ago. The Beta Israel of Ethiopia are also believed to be one of the Ten Lost Tribes of Israel.

Naomi Wadler

YOUTH ACTIVIST | b. OCTOBER 16, 2006 |
ADDIS ABABA, ETHIOPIA | ALEXANDRIA, VIRGINIA

NAOMI WADLER, a transracial adoptee born in Ethiopia, has always understood the power of listening to the voice deep inside of her. On the day of the Marjory Stoneman Douglas High School shooting in Parkland, Florida, eleven-year-old Naomi watched the news coverage from her mom's lap. Though she lived over a thousand miles away in Alexandria, Virginia, Naomi knew that she had to take action.

Naomi approached her friend in science class and they hatched a plan to join nationwide classroom walkouts to demand stricter gun laws. Unfortunately, their principal rejected their request, believing the protest was inappropriate for such young students. But Naomi was hoping for support, not permission, and she was ready to move forward without it. Naomi and her peers met on weekends and during recesses to organize every detail: writing petitions, making signs, creating press packets, and establishing community-wide agreements.

A week before the walkout, a Black student in Alabama named Courtlin Arrington was shot and killed in her classroom. Naomi was horrified to see that the shooting did not receive nearly the same media coverage as similar tragedies. Yet again, Naomi knew she had to do something. On the day of the walkout, two thousand five hundred schools across the country joined together in silence for seventeen minutes in honor of the seventeen Parkland students who lost their lives. But Naomi led her peers in silence for one additional minute—this time, to honor the Black girls and women who die by gun violence and are too often forgotten.

News of the walkout spread and soon Naomi was invited to stand in front of half a million people as the youngest speaker at the March for Our Lives rally in Washington, D.C. Her viral speech was just the beginning of Naomi's impact as an activist. But first? Celebrating her bat mitzvah! Naomi now advises a range of advocacy organizations across the country, even consulting on a new set of activist-minded American Girl dolls! As for what's next, Naomi dreams of becoming the first Ethiopian Jewish woman to serve as executive editor of the *New York Times*.

> "I represent the African American women who are victims of gun violence, who are simply statistics instead of vibrant, beautiful girls full of potential."

Jewish looks like... living by your convictions.

August Bondi

ABOLITIONIST, GUERILLA FIGHTER, JUDGE | 1833–1907
VIENNA, AUSTRIA | GREELEY, KANSAS

AUGUST BONDI was born a steadfast freedom fighter. As a young student in Vienna, he shook up his school by organizing over five hundred of his peers to boycott classes after a math teacher slapped one of the students. August made sure the boycott lasted until their teacher publicly apologized!

August's fight for justice continued to grow when his family moved to the United States in 1848. Within days of arriving in the Port of New Orleans, August began to witness the horrors of chattel slavery. He became a sailor on the Mississippi River and traveled to the Gulf of Mexico through Texas, where his desire to fight against the dehumanizing treatment of enslaved Black people intensified.

August was compelled by his Jewish values, which taught him to uphold and protect the freedoms of all people. So when the Kansas-Nebraska Act of 1854 declared that settlers in Kansas and Nebraska could decide whether free White people would be allowed to enslave Black people, August and other abolitionists raced into the territory to combat the spread of slavery. His solidarity didn't come without a cost. Proslavery fighters stole his horses and burned down his house.

Even when Kansas finally became a free state, August continued fighting against bondage. In fact, he volunteered his new family home as one of many safe houses for self-liberated people on the Underground Railroad! August was also one of the first to enlist in the Kansas Calvary and served the Union Army at the start of the Civil War. When the war ended, he rededicated himself to his community, serving as a judge, postmaster, and even a member of the local school board.

Through his lifetime of travels far and wide, August was as dedicated to Judaism as he was to abolitionism. He even wrote in his diary about celebrating Rosh Hashanah as a guest in a Jewish home . . . in the middle of the Civil War! Over a hundred years after his death, August Bondi remains an exemplar not only for Jews, but also for anyone who fights for freedom.

ANTI-RACISM

Today, August Bondi would be known as an anti-racist ally. A person who is anti-racist strives to fight against racism and White supremacy and puts their words into action. As an ally, August used his privilege and power to fight against slavery and support the Black community.

setting out menorahs
on tribal land.

Raquel Montoya-Lewis

ASSOCIATE JUSTICE OF THE WASHINGTON SUPREME COURT
b. APRIL 3, 1968 | SPAIN | PUEBLO OF ISLETA, NEW MEXICO | WASHINGTON

RAQUEL MONTOYA-LEWIS has tenacity running through her veins. She was born in Spain to a Native American father of the Pueblo of Laguna tribe and an Australian and Jewish mother. Because of her dad's role in the US Air Force, Raquel traveled the world throughout her childhood. But it was back home on her family's New Mexico reservation where she pursued her passion for repairing our broken world for future generations.

Raquel, an enrolled member of the Pueblo Isleta Indian tribe, felt deeply connected to both her Jewish and Indigenous identities on the reservation. Just as Native Americans persisted in the face of genocide and forced assimilation, Jews have survived and held on to their own identity despite a deep history of persecution. From a young age, Raquel knew she was called upon to translate this legacy of resilience into actionable change in the world.

In the United States, Indigenous people are put in jail at nearly twice the rate of their White peers. Empowered by her mission to reimagine this inequitable justice system, Raquel graduated from law school and came home to serve as a tribal judge. Raquel eventually moved to Washington, where she led as a chief judge for tribes all around the region, including the Lummi Nation and the Nooksack Indian Tribe.

It is nearly unheard of for Indigenous tribal judges to join the state and federal court system in the United States. But that didn't intimidate Associate Justice Raquel Montoya-Lewis! She became the first Native American to serve on the Washington Supreme Court and only the second Native American on any supreme court in the nation. Raquel continues to blaze trails for future Indigenous justices through her stalwart commitment to mentorship and advocacy.

JEWISH JUSTICES

In 1916, **Louis Brandeis** became the first of eight Jewish justices to serve on the Supreme Court of the United States! This includes **Elana Kagan** and the late **Ruth Bader Ginsburg**, trailblazers for gender equality and women's rights.

7

"My father really instilled in me the importance of *recognizing that I came from people who persisted, people who were lucky enough to survive,* and that my existence is dependent upon those people's persistence and resilience. That's something I hope I pass on to my own children."

—RAQUEL MONTOYA LEWIS

Jewish looks like...
signing the Torah portion
from the bimah.

Marlee Matlin

ACTRESS, AUTHOR, ACTIVIST | b. AUGUST 24, 1965 | MORTON GROVE, ILLINOIS

MARLEE MATLIN knew from a young age that if you can see it, you can be it. Marlee was raised in Morton Grove, Illinois, by hearing parents with Russian and Polish Ashkenazi Jewish roots and became deaf due to illness at eighteen months old. One day she was watching TV and saw a Deaf actor communicating with American Sign Language. Marlee was starstruck! If this Deaf person could make a career of acting, why couldn't she?

While Marlee performed locally in pursuit of her eventual Hollywood dreams, she attended Congregation Bene Shalom, the only full-service synagogue in the country dedicated to serving the Deaf and hard of hearing. Marlee studied Hebrew phonetically and became a bat mitzvah, reciting her Torah portion with both sign language and speech.

After a childhood of hustling for opportunities, Marlee landed a starring role in her first ever movie, *Children of a Lesser God* . . . and won an Academy Award! At twenty-one, Marlee was not only the youngest person to ever win the award for Best Actress, but also the first ever Deaf person to win an Oscar in any category.

As one of the most prominent Deaf actors in entertainment, Marlee uses her visibility to change the game for all those who follow in her footsteps. At the age of ten, when she realized all television programs weren't closed-captioned, making them inaccessible for the Deaf community, Marlee wrote a letter to President Gerald Ford demanding change. More than two decades later, she testified on Capitol Hill and was successful in getting federal legislation passed in support of closed-captioning requirements for all!

Marlee centers collaboration in her advocacy, whether demanding fellow Deaf actors be cast in Deaf roles or supporting disability rights in encounters with law enforcement.

DEAF INCLUSION IN JEWISH SPACES

There are more innovative and creative approaches to engaging the Jewish Deaf community today than ever before. Some ways to establish inclusive services in Jewish spaces include providing ready access to interpreters, closed-captioning, virtual services, rabbinical education, and other supports. During Rosh Hashanah services, for example, some clergy symbolize the blowing of the shofar by inflating brightly colored balloons that vibrate with sound!

11

Jewish looks like... challenging your own community to make change from within.

Sandra Lawson

RABBI | b. OCTOBER 14, 1970 | ST. LOUIS, MISSOURI

SANDRA LAWSON, a Black, queer US Army veteran turned personal trainer, loved developing friendships with her clients at the gym. So when a client invited her to visit their LGBTQ+ inclusive synagogue, she delighted in tagging along. Sandra had never seen such a vibrant, welcoming community in a formal religious setting before! She felt at home, and was inspired to explore and ultimately convert to Judaism.

But even after officially becoming a member of the tribe, Sandra struggled to feel fully accepted in Jewish spaces. Sandra was regularly asked invasive questions about her own identity while working with Jewish organizations. It was as if many White and White-presenting Jews felt entitled to proof of her credentials before they were comfortable sharing Jewish settings together. Things didn't get better when Sandra began studying to become a Reconstructionist rabbi. After getting rejected for role after role, Sandra was explicitly told by one congregation that they weren't ready for a Black rabbi. When Sandra was finally ordained in 2018, she became the first openly gay, female, and Black rabbi in the world!

Sandra was eventually welcomed with open arms as a chaplain at Elon University in North Carolina. And after years of bringing students together in a campus setting, Sandra now serves as a thought leader within the formal ranks of the Reconstructionist movement at large. Sandra is passionate about—and famous for—meeting Jews exactly where they are in their lives, even if that's outside the formal boundaries of a synagogue. To the delight of her thousands of online followers, this often takes the form of playful acoustic guitar riffs on social media or bite-sized Torah lessons on her podcast.

With her own lived experiences fueling her work, Rabbi Sandra is a celebrated powerhouse in dismantling racism and biases within Jewish communities. Sandra teaches that centering racial justice is a means of welcoming all Jews while disrupting White supremacy, the driving force of antisemitism.

BIBLICAL STORY OF RUTH

The biblical figure Ruth is one of the most famous Jewish converts of all time, touching many for her pride in Jewish peoplehood and her acts of courage. She exemplifies how Jews come from a range of diverse backgrounds and are bound as one people through shared purpose and tradition.

Jewish looks like...
**turning dreams
into reality
for yourself and
bringing
others along.**

Ezra Frech

PARALYMPIC ATHLETE | b. MAY 11, 2005 | LOS ANGELES, CALIFORNIA

LIKE MANY LITTLE KIDS, Ezra Frech loved playing sports. In fact, his first word wasn't "mama" or "doggy," it was "BALL!" One thing set him apart from many other sports-loving kids, though. Ezra had congenital limb differences and was born without his left knee, left calf bone, and fingers on his left hand. However, this didn't stop Ezra! Before his first birthday, Ezra had already received his first prosthetic leg and learned to pull himself up to stand. After spending hours in surgeries and physical therapy throughout his childhood, he was better able to move comfortably in his prosthetics.

Even though Ezra was the only kid in his entire school with a visible disability, he felt destined to become a star athlete. He played basketball, baseball, soccer, football, practiced karate, and even learned math through sports. What better way to count by twos than by adding up shots during basketball games? With the devoted support of his parents, Ezra pursued his dreams of becoming a professional athlete and set his sights on the high jump, long jump, and one hundred meters. When he was only fourteen years old, Ezra became the youngest athlete in the world to compete in the 2019 World Para Athletics Championships, making it all the way to the finals in each of his three track-and-field events. And only a year later, he competed as the youngest US athlete in the 2020 Paralympic Games in Tokyo!

But for Ezra, it was never just about his own athletic dreams. He was raised to value community, something he learned from his Jewish mother, who fled the Iranian Revolution as a child. This passion led Ezra and his family to create their own nonprofit organization, called Angel City Sports, which provides sports opportunities, equipment, and coaching for disabled people of all ages. The Angel City Games are one of the largest adapted sports organizations in the country, bringing together kids, wounded warriors, elite disabled athletes, and more to compete in community. Ezra's future is bright not only because of his elite athleticism, but also because of his commitment to creating opportunities for disabled people everywhere.

HIGHLIGHTING JEWISH PARALYMPIC ATHLETES

Ezra Frech is an outstanding athlete, and he's also in good Jewish company! Fellow Jewish athletes who compete with a range of physical disabilities, also known as Paralympians, include **Matthew Levy**, an Australian swimmer with cerebral palsy, and Asian American table tennis player **Ian Seidenfeld**, who was born with pseudoachondroplasia dwarfism. Even the founder of the Paralympic Games was the German Jewish doctor **Ludwig Guttman**!

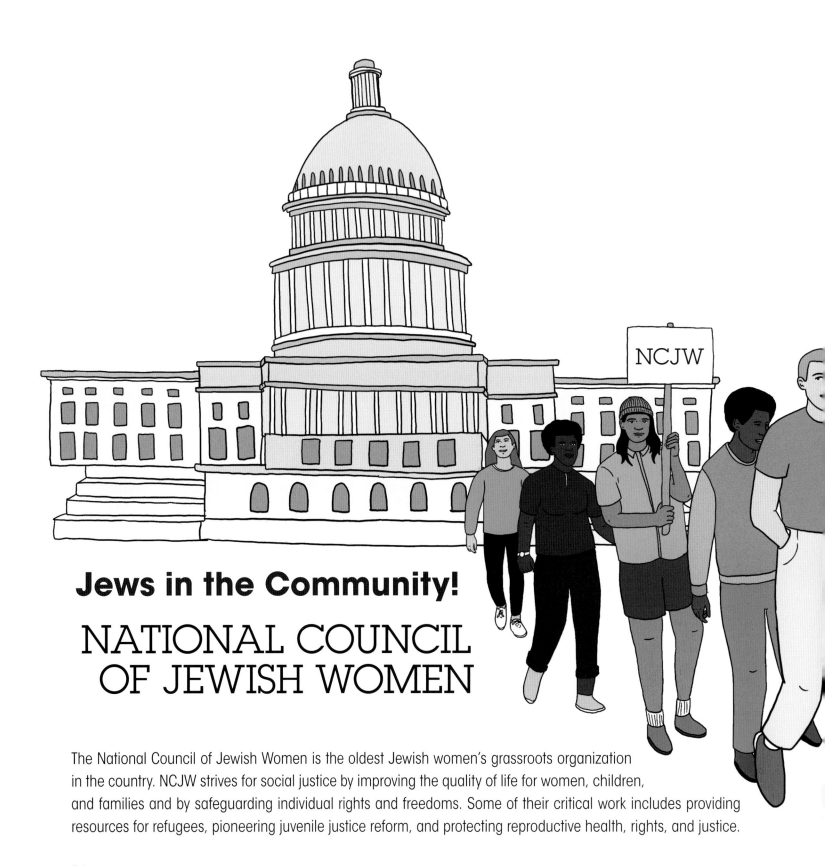

Jews in the Community!

NATIONAL COUNCIL OF JEWISH WOMEN

The National Council of Jewish Women is the oldest Jewish women's grassroots organization in the country. NCJW strives for social justice by improving the quality of life for women, children, and families and by safeguarding individual rights and freedoms. Some of their critical work includes providing resources for refugees, pioneering juvenile justice reform, and protecting reproductive health, rights, and justice.

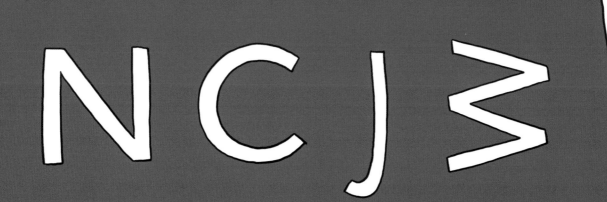

"*Jewish looks like . . .*
love, community, and collective
work for a more just world."

**Rabbi Danya Ruttenberg,
Scholar in Residence at the
National Council of Jewish Women**

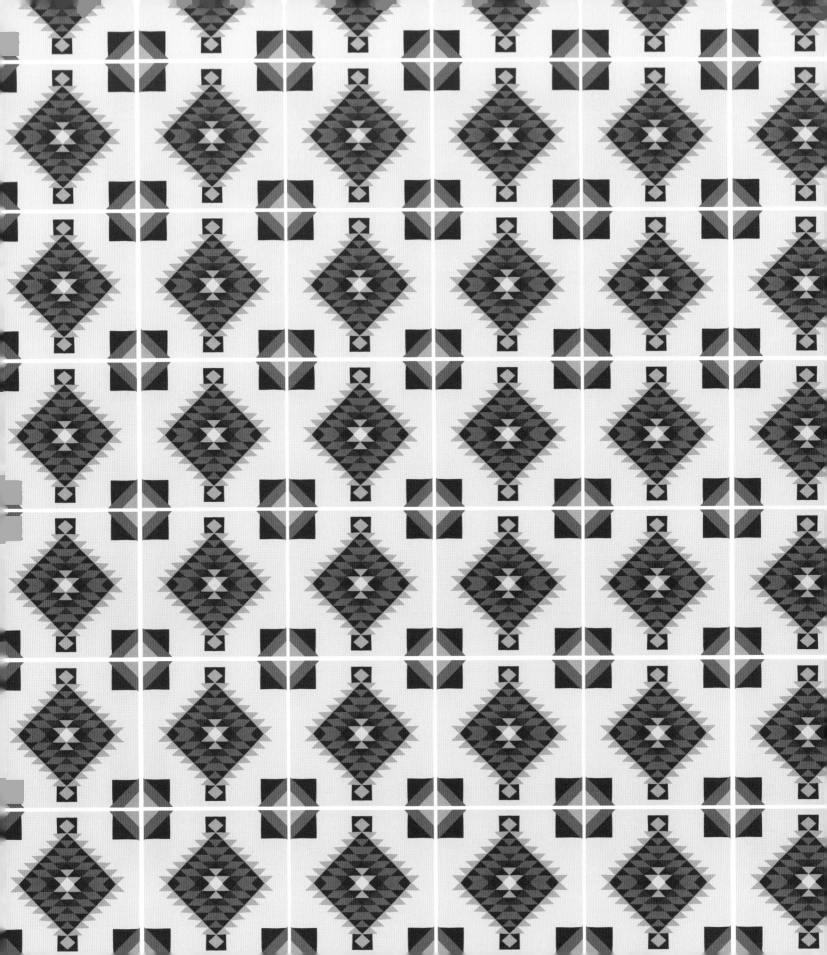

אמץ לב

OMETZ LEV

COURAGE

Jewish looks like...

being "Black by birth,
a Jew by choice, and
a revolutionary by necessity."

Charles McDew

ACTIVIST, PROFESSOR | JUNE 23, 1938–APRIL 3, 2018 | MASSILLON, OHIO

GROWING UP in Ohio during the Jim Crow era, Charles McDew was no stranger to discrimination. He also wasn't a stranger to doing something about it. When he was in eighth grade, Charles was already participating in local protests supporting the religious freedom of Amish students. Bigotry was an all-too-familiar reality for his own family, too. Despite having taught chemistry back in South Carolina, Charles's father couldn't find a teaching job in Ohio because he was Black. Instead, he went to work in the steel mill.

When it was time for Charles to head off to college, he chose the HBCU South Carolina State College. Unfortunately, racist encounters in college made it far from a safe haven for learning. Charles was unjustly arrested three times in two days: once for fighting back when an officer struck him for not calling him "sir," once for refusing to sit in the "Blacks only" baggage car on the train, and once for taking a shortcut through a "Whites only" park. The bigotry Charles faced directly contributed to him joining the Jewish faith. After being denied entrance to a White Christian church, Charles converted to Judaism, where he found a welcome home.

JEWS AND HISTORICALLY BLACK COLLEGES AND UNIVERSITIES (HBCU)

After Adolf Hitler's rise to power, many intellectuals fled Europe to the United States. But antisemitism was prevalent on America's shores, too, and many Jewish refugees struggled to find jobs. Some of the few places that welcomed Jewish professors and scholars were HBCUs. Administrators supported German Jewish scholars by offering them jobs at HBCUs and preventing their deportation!

Charles responded to his arrests by becoming a founder of the Student Non-violent Coordinating Committee (SNCC), a group dedicated to using nonviolent methods to fight for racial justice. Their organized activism, such as the Woolworth lunch counter sit-ins, showed the world the power of young people! His fellow students were eager for Charles to take the lead and organize sit-ins at local segregated businesses. At first Charles declined, but then was inspired by Hillel's famous quote: "If not me, who? If not now, when?" Charles was all in.

Charles continued to fight for civil rights throughout his career as a teacher, labor organizer, and community activist. In the wake of Charles's death, the National Association for the Advancement of Colored People (NAACP) issued a statement that honored his "central role in mobilizing young people across the South at the height of the Civil Rights Movement." Charles McDew set the bar for what student activism can look like even to this day.

Jewish looks like...
**flying the rainbow flag
over city hall.**

Harvey Milk

POLITICIAN, CIVIL RIGHTS ACTIVIST | MAY 22, 1930–NOVEMBER 27, 1978
WOODMERE, NEW YORK | SAN FRANCISCO, CALIFORNIA

HARVEY MILK proved that hope takes root in loud, relentless community action. But Harvey wasn't always vocal about his beliefs, or even his own identity. He was born to Lithuanian Jewish immigrants in Woodmere, New York, where his grandfather founded the local synagogue. Harvey knew from a young age that he was gay, but he kept it private for fear of his conservative family's response. He was even forced to resign from the military in 1955 when his superiors suspected him of being gay.

That all changed when he moved to San Francisco. Harvey joined the proud, bustling LGBTQ+ community in the Castro neighborhood and never looked back. In 1973, only one year after moving to California, Harvey decided to run for a seat on the San Francisco Board of Supervisors. Harvey opened a camera store called Castro Camera that served as his lively, volunteer-filled campaign headquarters. He even hung his bar mitzvah picture front and center on the wall!

Harvey got right to work pushing back against inequity through coalition-building. When beer distributors refused to allow drivers to unionize, he connected gay bar owners and Arab and Chinese grocers to successfully stage a boycott. When the local merchants association tried to prevent two gay men from opening an antique shop, Harvey organized the Castro Village Association so that LGBTQ+-owned businesses could collectively make their voices heard.

Whether at a protest, march, or bus stop, Harvey spoke passionately about the importance of visibility and collective action for all who are disenfranchised. The queer community is not a monolith, and some of Harvey's tactics to shine a light on queer heroes caused harm. This includes Harvey's decision to out Oliver Sipple, the then-closeted bystander who prevented an assassination attempt against President Gerald Ford.

Harvey lost three elections in a row, but never gave up the fight. Finally, in 1977, Harvey Milk was elected supervisor, making him the first openly gay elected public official in California. He soon sponsored and passed a civil rights bill preventing discrimination on the basis of sexual orientation in housing, employment, and public accommodations. Tragically, eleven months after Harvey entered office, he and San Francisco Mayor George Moscone were assassinated by a fellow city supervisor. Though his political career and life were cut far too short, Harvey Milk, the unofficial Mayor of Castro Street, is remembered today as a revolutionary icon of hope. In fact, his birthday, May 22, is celebrated across California as Harvey Milk Day.

GAY PRIDE SYMBOLS: FROM PINK TRIANGLES TO THE RAINBOW FLAG

During the Holocaust, the Nazis forced gay men to wear upside-down pink triangles. While this label was meant to further dehumanize prisoners, the LGBTQ+ community reclaimed the symbol in the 1970s as a badge of liberation. Once Harvey Milk was elected as a supervisor, he approached artist Gilbert Baker, a gay man and drag queen, with a challenge: Could Gilbert create a new symbol of gay pride for the community? Soon after Harvey issued the challenge, Gilbert designed, sewed, and flew the very first rainbow flag!

Itzhak Perlman

VIOLINIST, CONDUCTOR | b. AUGUST 31, 1945
TEL AVIV-YAFO, ISRAEL (THEN BRITISH MANDATE OF PALESTINE)

ITZHAK PERLMAN was only three years old when he heard a classical violinist on the radio and fell in love with music. He was determined to play the violin himself but was promptly rejected by the local conservatory because he was too small to hold the instrument. Instead of deterring him, it lit a fire within young Itzhak. With that fire, he taught himself how to play the violin . . . on a toy fiddle! This experience helped form an early belief that continues to guide Itzhak's life: people should be judged for what they can do, not by what they can't.

Only one year later, Itzhak contracted polio and lost his ability to walk without support. Again, Itzhak was committed to pursuing his passion for music even when medical and musical experts were sure he would fail. His parents had emigrated from Poland as anti-Jewish sentiment built before World War II, which meant Itzhak had access to the Tel Aviv Academy of Music. When talent scouts from *The Ed Sullivan Show* went in search of acts for the variety show, they became enamored with Itzhak. The scouts flew thirteen-year-old Itzhak all the way to New York to play live on the show. He was a smash sensation! Itzhak's performance was a striking turning point that launched his trailblazing career.

Itzhak is known for his dynamic interpretation of music and engaging rapport with his audience. He has performed everywhere from President Barack Obama's inauguration to the field of his beloved New York Mets. He's won sixteen Grammy Awards, including the Lifetime Achievement Award in 2008. And the hauntingly heartbreaking theme song from *Schindler's List*? That's Itzhak working his magic on the violin! After winning the one-million-dollar Genesis Prize, he dedicated the money to increasing inclusion of people with disabilities across Jewish life.

In the mind of the world's most famous violinist, one thing has not changed ever since his childhood. Itzhak Perlman is not heroic for using his scooter or braces and crutches to get to the stage. What matters most of all is what happens once he is there: making music.

JEWISH STRINGED MUSIC

Itzhak Perlman plays the four-string violin in other contexts beyond classical, including klezmer music, which is a traditional Eastern European style. A range of stringed instruments have always played a central role in Jewish music, whether the seven-string Turkish saz, the seventy-eight-string Arabic qanun, or ten-string kinnor from biblical times!

"I couldn't shed my Jewish identity any more than I could shed being a woman or being Korean. It was not just a part of my DNA,

but it was the way
I look at the whole world.
It was who I was
in every fiber of
my being."

—ANGELA WARNICK
BUCHDAHL

Jewish looks like...
adding kimchi on the Seder plate.

Angela Warnick Buchdahl

RABBI | b. JULY 8, 1972 | SEOUL, KOREA | NEW YORK, NEW YORK

ANGELA WARNICK BUCHDAHL knows that inclusivity makes her own Jewish identity stronger. She was born in Seoul, South Korea, to a Korean Buddhist mom and American Jewish father and moved to Tacoma, Washington, when she was nearly five years old. She loved making big, delicious Korean meals for Jewish holy days like Shabbat. On one Passover, her family even swapped kimchi for maror on the Seder plate!

But not everyone felt the same way as Angela. Growing up, she and her sister were the only Asian kids at synagogue and Jewish summer camp. The first time she traveled to Israel, other kids questioned whether she was really Jewish. Angela was exhausted from constantly defending her Jewish identity. For a brief moment, she thought about leaving Judaism altogether. But instead of believing the harmful things that others said, Angela rose above them.

Once she set her mind to becoming a Jewish leader, Angela was off! Right after graduating from college, she enrolled at Hebrew Union College. At the investiture ceremony, Angela became the first ever Asian American cantor. And just two years later, she became the first ever Asian American rabbi! Another first? Rabbi Buchdahl is the first woman to lead from the storied New York's Central Synagogue's bimah in its one-hundred-eight-year history. It's here where she sets a vision that centers inclusivity and connection above all else. Angela teaches that Jewish peoplehood is about being a family bound through not just bloodline, but also adoption, conversion, shared values, and more. Rabbi Buchdahl's message and leadership has resonated across the country, and she's been widely recognized for her leadership in both the Asian and Jewish communities. She was named by *Newsweek* as one of the "Top Fifty Most Influential Rabbis in America," and in 2021, she received the Asia Game Changer Award. While Angela is proud to be the first in many areas of her life, her mentorship and advocacy chart a path forward for countless others.

On January 16, 2022, a gunman held a rabbi and three congregants hostage inside a synagogue in Colleyville, Texas. The man then called Rabbi Buchdahl, a leader of a synagogue over fifteen hundred miles away, to demand she use her influence to release a terrorist from a Texas prison. Rabbi Buchdahl remained steady and all hostages eventually escaped. However, this painful incident reveals the real-life dangers of antisemitic conspiracies claiming that Jews are all-powerful.

Jewish looks like...
transforming pain
into art.

Anish Kapoor

SCULPTOR | b. MARCH 12, 1954 | BOMBAY (NOW MUMBAI), INDIA | LONDON, ENGLAND

SCULPTOR ANISH KAPOOR knows what it feels like to juggle different identities. Growing up in Mumbai to a Punjabi Hindu father and an Iraqi Jewish mother, Anish spent his early years struggling to fit into Indian society.

When Anish was seventeen, he and his brother boarded a plane for Israel, where they worked on a kibbutz. Though his time in Israel was difficult in many ways, he appreciated being part of a community where people helped and supported one another. It was there that he had a fleeting goal of becoming an engineer, until he soon realized that he wasn't passionate or skilled enough at math. Instead, Anish decided he would pursue art, something he'd loved since childhood.

With his mind set, Anish hitchhiked across Europe until he arrived in London to attend art school. His career has flourished on the international stage ever since! Anish is known for creating enormous sculptures of different shapes, colors, and materials. The famous Cloud Gate in Downtown Chicago, the one that's in the shape of a sixty-six-foot-long stainless-steel bean? That is Anish's very own work!

Even though he has won many awards and accolades on the international stage, Anish has never forgotten his Jewish roots. His Shoah Memorial was dedicated on the fifty-eighth anniversary of Kristallnacht (Night of the Broken Glass) and sits in the Liberal Jewish Synagogue in London. Unfortunately, in 2015 his sculpture Dirty Corner at the Palace of Versailles in France was vandalized with antisemitic graffiti. Anish wanted to leave the graffiti to remind people that antisemitism and racism are ever-present in our society, but local French authorities forced him to remove it. In the end, he decided to cover the graffiti in gold leaf to turn the harm into something positive and healing, while never forgetting the pain underneath.

To this day, Anish continues to create stunning works of art. His vision brings communities together, a dream from his days on the kibbutz finally coming true. Though he used to be a little boy who felt stuck between cultures, Anish has transformed into an artist with the ability to tell stories and share messages that resonate with people around the world.

Anish won the one-million-dollar Genesis Prize, which recognizes Jewish talent and achievement. Anish directed his winnings toward five prominent nonprofits working to alleviate the global refugee crisis, one of which is helping Syrian refugees. In his own words, "Like many Jews, I do not have to go far back in my family history to find people who were refugees. Directing Genesis Prize funds to this cause is a way of helping people who, like my forebears not too long before them, are fleeing persecution."

Jewish looks like...
defying tradition to build
something better.

Osnat Barzani

RABBI | 1590–1670 | MOSUL, KURDISTAN (IRAQ)

IT TAKES MANY SKILLS to be a successful rabbi. You need to be committed to Judaism, of course, but also knowledgeable about the Torah. And you need to take great care of your community. As the world's first ever female rabbi, Osnat Barzani was all of the above, and more!

Osnat was born over four hundred years ago in Mosul, Kurdistan, which today is known as Iraq. Her father was a well-known and respected rabbi named Shmuel b. Netanel Ha-Levi. He built a school called a yeshiva in Mosul, where young men would come and study the Talmud. Most fathers did not allow their daughters to attend school, but not Osnat's dad! Rabbi Shmuel was impressed by his daughter's brain and spirit and trained her to become a scholar. He even made her future husband promise that he would allow Osnat to focus on her studies instead of housework. When Osnat's husband died, it was Osnat who became the new rabbinical teacher!

Osnat was beloved as a sage in her community. This adoration was in no small part due to her possessing mastery of Jewish texts, which she taught to rooms full of male rabbinical students. Osnat was even given the rare and honorable title of Tanna'it, which is the female form of a Talmudic scholar.

Beyond her exceptional rabbinical knowledge, there were also stories about Osnat possessing mystical powers. These were passed down by Kurdish Jews filling their amulets with folklore about Osnat's life. Many believed that she was able to communicate with her deceased father through her dreams, especially to protect the community. On one trip to Amedi during the holiday of Rosh Hodesh, Osnat persuaded the congregation to celebrate outside the synagogue together under the starry sky. Soon after, a fire broke out inside the synagogue! No one was harmed, all because of Osnat's foresight. Even the Torah scrolls were saved, and the grateful community renamed their synagogue after her. Centuries later, Osnat's legacy lives on as inspiration for Jewish women around the world.

WOMEN RABBINICAL LEADERS

Osnat may have been the first female rabbi, but she certainly wasn't the last! While many assume that men have always been the ones to lead congregations, times have thankfully changed. There are currently over twelve hundred female rabbis worldwide, who belong to different Jewish denominations, and that number is only increasing!

Jews in the Community!

CAMP BE'CHOL LASHON

Be'chol Lashon (Hebrew for "in every language") strengthens Jewish identity by raising awareness about the ethnic, racial, and cultural diversity of Jewish identity and experience. Be'chol Lashon offers diversity training workshops, educational resources, and a multi-cultural overnight camp called Camp Be'chol Lashon that teaches about global Jewish diversity.

"Jewish looks like . . .
having the strength and support
to tell our own multicultural, multiracial stories,
and the enthusiastic affirmation
that they're each authentically Jewish."

**Julian Voloj,
Chief Operating Officer of Be'chol Lashon**

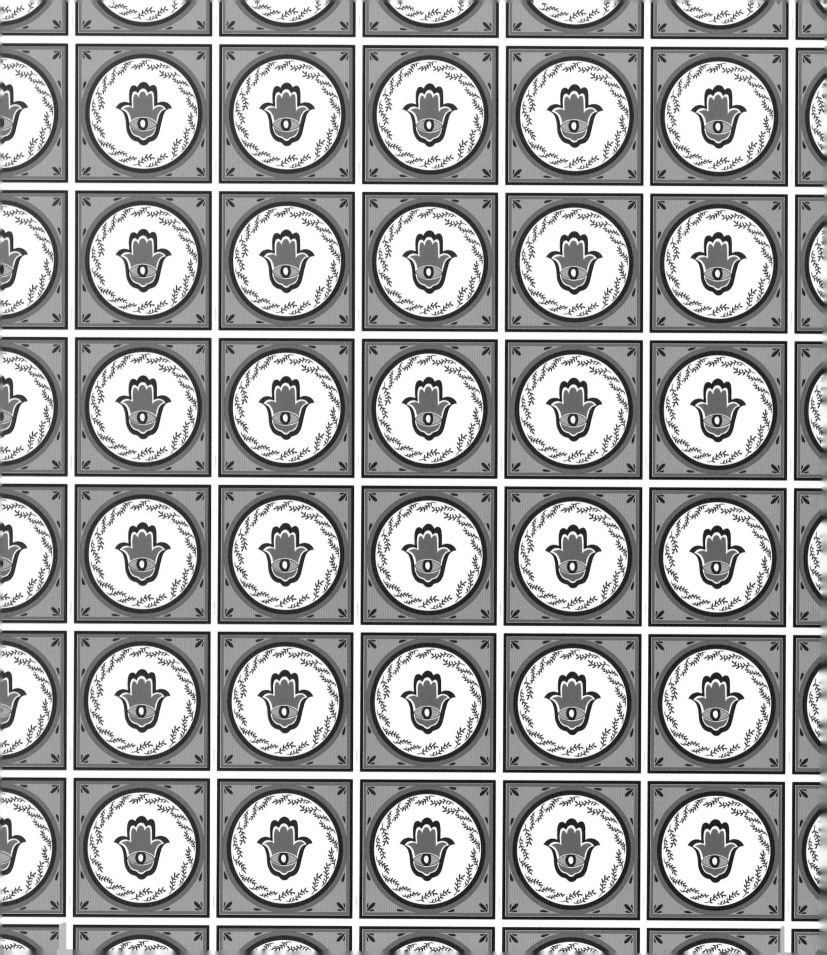

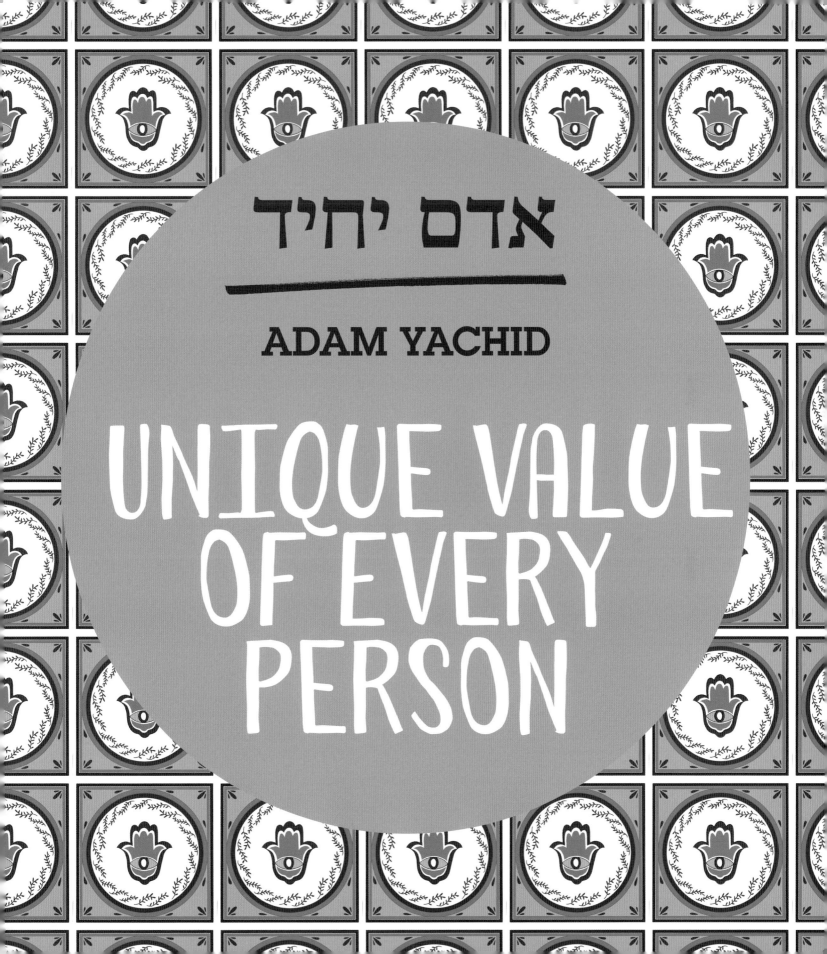

Victor "Young" Perez

BOXER | OCTOBER 18, 1911–JANUARY 21, 1945
DAR-EL BERDGANA, TUNISIA | PARIS, FRANCE

THEY SAY don't judge a book by its cover, and Victor "Young" Perez proved you shouldn't judge a boxer by their size, either. Victor grew up as one of five kids in the impoverished Jewish quarter of Tunis, Dar-El Berdgana. Even though he only ever reached five feet, two inches, Victor spent his childhood boxing all the other kids in his neighborhood . . . and winning.

Victor moved to Paris at seventeen to chase his dreams of becoming a boxing champion. Despite rising antisemitism throughout Europe, Victor proudly wore a Star of David on his shorts during each and every competition. It only took a few years of international competition before he faced the American boxer Frankie Genaro in pursuit of the 1931 World Flyweight crown . . . and won! At age twenty, Victor officially became the youngest world champion in the history of boxing. He was living a life of freedom and fame, and eventually retired with an impressive one hundred thirty-eight career fights, ninety-two wins, and twenty-nine wins by knockout.

But everything changed as the German army occupied Paris at the onset of World War II. In 1943, Victor became one of one thousand Jews sent to the Auschwitz concentration camp in the infamous "Transport 60." Victor was forced to perform slave labor in a factory kitchen and, in an act of defiance and solidarity, he regularly sneaked crates of soup to his friends hiding in the alley with empty bowls.

Officers knew of Victor's illustrious career and exploited his fame for their own entertainment. They forced Victor to box in matches against fellow prisoners. But when Victor was made to fight—and ultimately knocked out—an SS officer, he was prohibited from boxing ever again. Only weeks before Auschwitz was liberated, the Nazis led thirty-three-year-old Victor and others on a death march to a camp farther east. When Victor discovered abandoned bread and attempted to distribute it to the others, he was murdered by an officer.

Today, Victor is celebrated for his boxing legacy and has been inducted into the International Jewish Sports Hall of Fame. He is remembered not only for his athletic prowess but also for his courage and tenacity in the face of hatred.

PERSECUTION OF JEWS IN NORTH AFRICA DURING THE HOLOCAUST

While many assume that only European Jews were impacted by the Holocaust, the horrors spread far beyond one continent. Nearly half a million Jews lived across North Africa during the war and were affected by pro-Nazi regimes in countries like Morocco and Algeria, as well as the German occupation of Tunisia and Libya.

Bill Pinkney

SAILOR | SEPTEMBER 15, 1935–AUGUST 31, 2023 | CHICAGO, IL

BILL PINKNEY knew early on that commitment would be the driving force in his life. He watched his single mother work tirelessly to provide for him and his sister on the South Side of Chicago. When his seventh grade teacher encouraged him to read *Call It Courage*, Bill was transfixed by the protagonist's determination to prove himself by setting sail alone on the ocean. Bill felt this same call to prove himself. He wondered if he, too, could commit to his dream of sailing around the world on his own!

Bill's love of the water brought him to the United States Navy where, despite encountering racism, he served for eight years as a hospital corpsman. But he never forgot his childhood dream and finally decided to pursue it at all costs. Bill collaborated with the Chicago and Boston public school systems so that students could track his voyage while he recorded educational content from the sea. He wanted every single child to know that they were worthy of ocean-sized goals, and he was set on using his own journey to help crack open their belief in themselves.

On August 5, 1990, after years of training and preparation, Bill set sail from Boston Harbor alone on his boat that he proudly named none other than *Commitment*. Back home, students eagerly followed his every move via the boat's transmitter that sent location updates each day. In order to circumnavigate the globe, Bill needed to successfully round all five great capes, including the particularly treacherous Cape Horn in South America. Massive waves, strong currents, and turbulent winds nearly destroyed Pinkney's boat! After twenty-two months and 32,000 miles, Captain Bill Pinkney sailed back into Boston Harbor to thousands of students, educators, and community members welcoming him home. Captain Bill Pinkney was officially the first Black man to sail solo around the world!

Bill spent the remainder of his life educating others about community building and human rights through his sailing. He served as the first captain of the *Amistad* replica, the enslaved persons transport vessel, and took schoolteachers to West Africa on a route tracing the Middle Passage. Pinkney's life is a testament to the truths he held most dear: that our collective freedom is intertwined, and that we must commit ourselves to serving one another.

> Bill felt a strong pull to Judaism as a child and eventually converted as an adult. In times of uncertainty and fear while sailing dangerous waters, he often turned to Psalm 107: "Then they cry unto the Lord in their trouble, and he bringeth them out of their distresses. He maketh the storm a calm, so that the waves thereof are still."

41

Jewish looks like... writing your own story as an act of resistance.

Tracee Ellis Ross

ACTOR, COMEDIAN, ENTREPRENEUR | b. OCTOBER 29, 1972 | LOS ANGELES, CALIFORNIA

TRACEE ELLIS ROSS knows a thing or two about the importance of charting your own path. She spent her childhood watching her Black superstar mother, Diana Ross, do just that in the music industry. While Tracee had a larger-than-life personality and big aspirations of her own, she wasn't always sure how to channel her gifts into writing her personal story.

Tracee had her big break in the sitcom *Girlfriends*, where she got to show off her Jewish comedic chops, which she learned from her father, Robert Ellis Silberstein. While Tracee celebrated the sitcom as a powerful success story, particularly within Black communities, she was struck that it never reached wider audiences. This was one of many times Tracee would experience firsthand how Black women and their stories are often shrugged off and undervalued by Hollywood.

It lit a fire that guided Tracee toward her beloved role as the matriarch in the hit ABC show *Black-ish*. No topic was too big for the show and cast, and episodes tackled everything from police brutality to inadequate White allyship. Tracee was so impactful that, in 2017, she became the first Black woman in over thirty years to receive a nomination for a Golden Globe in the Best Actress in a Television Series Musical or Comedy category . . . and she won!

Learning to value her own voice unlocked Tracee's desire to advocate for the layered, dynamic stories of Black women everywhere. She collaborated with Oprah Winfrey to produce and host the limited series *The Hair Tales*, which is a joyful celebration of Black women told through the lens of their hair journeys. This passion also extended to her role as founder of Pattern, a bestselling hair care company that caters directly to the full range of Black, textured hair.

Whether developing award-winning characters, boundary-breaking companies, or hilarious videos on social media, Tracee owns her power and channels it toward the collective good. As a Black and Jewish woman, she knows that self-advocacy takes courage. And Tracee Ellis Ross's unstoppable courage has proven to be a form of resistance in and of itself.

> "This is for all of the women, women of color and colorful people, whose stories, ideas, thoughts are not always considered worthy and valid and important. But I want you to know that I see you. We see you."

JEWISH HUMOR

Jews and humor go together like apples and honey. While Jews constitute only 2 percent of the US population, a *Time* article from 1978 estimated that 80 percent of the country's professional comedians at that time were Jewish! For a people whose history is riddled with persecution and pain, humor extends beyond a good

chuckle—it's often a means of survival. This uniquely Jewish brand of humor is known for conjuring up imagery of the "old country" shtetl, self-referential jokes, and an anti-authoritarianism streak. But as a diverse range of humorists add their voices to the collective canon, our understanding of Jewish humor is evolving from exclusively Ashkenazi-centric content to a more inclusive art form.

It's about time!

Jewish looks like...
living to see a
world filled with
joyous liberation.

Is Perlman

STUDENT, ACTIVIST, ARTIST | b. JULY 9, 2003 | MIAMI, FLORIDA

TRANSGENDER AND NON-BINARY

student and artist Is Perlman grew up as a cheerful kid in a loving home in Florida. But while Is's parents supported their transition, the rest of the world was not as understanding. The never-ending flood of anti-trans rhetoric and policies, both in Florida and across the country, took a toll on Is's mental health. The once confident child soon felt shame in their own skin. Unfortunately, traditional Jewish gatherings didn't offer relief. As a multiracial Asian American Jew, Is already felt apprehensive in formal, pre-dominantly White Jewish spaces. Owning their queer identity on top of their racial identity felt even more out of reach.

Is designed a face mask for the Broadway show What the Constitution Means to Me, which was then sold to raise money for the grassroots Black Trans Travel Fund.

But things started to change when Is attended a Shabbaton retreat organized by Keshet, a Jewish LGBTQ+ advocacy nonprofit. There were Jewish prayers that not only accepted, but celebrated, Is's trans body as holy! Is finally felt a deep connection that helped bolster their mental healing and wellness. They now refuse to let the hate of others dictate how they love themselves. Is became an active student leader within the very same community organization, offering other kids like them opportunities for authentic connection. After leading the LGBTQ+ Jewish Youth of Color Collective, Is went on to successfully advocate for a gender-neutral bathroom in their school! They were part of the first group of students to present at a district-wide conference in Miami-Dade County on how teachers can best support queer and trans students.

Is knows that reclaiming their creativity is itself an act of defiance. Their art—full of performance pieces, photography, paintings, and poetry—weaves together Jewish traditions and trans experiences while challenging the suffering that so often dominates trans narratives. Another act of celebratory defiance? Is was named a 2021 US Presidential Scholar in the Arts, one of the country's highest honors for young artists!

Is continues to use their voice to advocate for trans-affirming communities and legislation. Most transformational of all, they do so by centering trans joy and liberation every step of the way.

Jewish looks like...
creating mashups that make way for inclusivity.

Daveed Diggs

ACTOR, WRITER, RAPPER | b. JANUARY 24, 1982 | OAKLAND, CALIFORNIA

DURING HIS CHILDHOOD in Oakland, California, Daveed Diggs knew that some people viewed his parents as coming from two separate, incompatible worlds: his mom is a White Jewish social worker and his dad is a Black non-Jewish bus driver. But Daveed never saw it that way. He embraced his multiracial and multi-religious family fully, never feeling just half of anything.

In fact, Daveed has always been the king of mashups. He chased auditions across town in pursuit of his passion for rapping and acting. In order to make ends meet, he pieced together a range of classroom gigs like substitute teaching, even developing a rap curriculum used in Bay Area middle schools! Daveed intentionally blended as many creative mediums as possible. In fact, he found his big break when he joined a group that crosses improv with hip-hop. The group, Freestyle Love Supreme, was cofounded by Lin-Manuel Miranda. That's the same Lin-Manuel Miranda who created the breakout Broadway hit *Hamilton* . . . and who went on to hire Daveed to star in the original cast! Daveed sparkled on the stage and won a Tony Award for his groundbreaking portrayal of both the Marquis de Lafayette and Thomas Jefferson.

But perhaps the ultimate example of a Daveed Diggs–style mashup is the rap and klezmer song "Puppy for Hanukkah," which he created with his experimental hip-hop trio called Clipping. Kids around the world now bop along to the lyrics full of dreidel spinning, latke eating, and hysterically unconventional puppy-naming. The song even includes a full Hebrew blessing!

As Daveed continues to blend labels and genres in his own work, he creates spaces for others to show up fully as they are—both in the Jewish community and beyond. Growing up, Daveed felt accepted by the Jewish community for some parts of his identity but less so for others, including his experience as a Black man in America. Now, as an adult, his art actively resists this form of tokenism. Whether centering Black joy in Jewish holiday music or representing the American founders as men of color, Daveed is leading the charge toward innovation and inclusivity.

ALL I WANT FOR CHRISTMAS IS . . . JEWISH SONGWRITERS?

What do "Rudolph the Red-Nosed Reindeer," "Have Yourself a Merry Little Christmas," "Santa Baby," and "It's the Most Wonderful Time of the Year" all have in common? Yes, they're some of the best and most famous Christmas songs of all time. But they (and many other chart-topping hits) are also all written by Jews!

Jewish looks like...
becoming one of the greatest basketball players of all time.

Sue Bird

BASKETBALL PLAYER | b. OCTOBER 16, 1980 | SYOSSET, NEW YORK

SUE BIRD is known around the world as an unstoppable force. But growing up, being unstoppable often meant getting in trouble with her parents, a Russian Jewish dad and non-Jewish mom. Sue was the only girl playing pickup basketball against the boys on her Syosset, New York, neighborhood court. She would sink baskets and hone her signature no-look pass until it was too dark to see the ball, far past when her mom was calling her name for dinner.

Sue's unrelenting competitiveness took her straight to the top. Serving as point guard and captain, Sue led her high school teammates to the national title and her UConn college team to two NCAA national championships. It came as no surprise that, in 2002, only five years into the WNBA's existence, Sue was drafted as the first overall pick!

BASKETBALL AND JEWISH QUOTAS

Basketball was invented in the late nineteenth century and was celebrated as a beloved sport among immigrant Jewish youth in New York. In the 1920s, however, Harvard University and many other universities instituted de facto quotas for Jewish student university enrollment to address what Harvard's president termed the "Jew problem." Yale University's alumni successfully came together to demand an end to these discriminatory practices, in no small part due to their desire to win more games, given Jewish excellence in basketball. This marked a turning point in Jewish American inclusion and acceptance in higher education.

Though Sue played for the Seattle Storm for her entire nineteen-season career, basketball has taken her all over the world: China, Turkey, Russia, France, Australia, Croatia, and beyond. She even briefly lived in Tel Aviv, where she gained her Israeli citizenship. Sue earned so many accolades over her world-traveling career that she's known as one of the most decorated players in the history of basketball, regardless of gender: five hundred fifty-nine career starts, thirteen WNBA All-Star selections, five consecutive Olympic gold medals, four WNBA championships, and four FIBA World Cup wins. It's no wonder Sue was selected as one of the two flag bearers for the United States during the opening ceremonies at the Tokyo Olympics!

But Sue's relentlessness extends far beyond the court. She knew that her starting salary was only 1 percent of the average man's NBA salary. Rather than accept the status quo, Sue used her platform and leadership in the player's union to influence a new collective bargaining agreement and increase player salaries. When the WNBA dedicated its 2020 season to Black Lives Matter, Sue helped to establish visible social justice messages and policies everywhere, from jerseys to the court. Sue came out publicly as a lesbian in 2017, and she and soccer superstar wife, Megan Rapinoe, are unrelenting advocates for the LGBTQ+ community. Though Sue retired after her 2022 season as the oldest player in the WNBA, she continues to be an unstoppable force for good in the world.

Jews in the Community!
JEWS OF COLOR INITIATIVE

The Jews of Color Initiative advances racial equity in the US Jewish community by centering the leadership of Jews of Color and ensuring that communities and institutions reflect the multiracial reality of the Jewish people. Their nonprofit advocacy works include generating groundbreaking research, grant making, and community education, as well as supporting leaders, amplifying best practices, and advancing policies that strengthen the multiracial Jewish community.

"Jewish looks like . . . kippot tucked tight under fitted caps so brothers don't drop them as they dabke and bounce."

**Ilana Kaufman,
Chief Executive Officer
of Jews of Color
Initiative**

פקוח נפש

PIKUACH NEFESH

TO SAVE
A LIFE

Jewish looks like...
turning oppression into
a Nobel-prize discovery.

Rita Levi-Montalcini

SCIENTIST (NEUROEMBRYOLOGIST) | APRIL 22, 1909–DECEMBER 30, 2012 | TURIN, ITALY

RITA LEVI-MONTALCINI was no stranger to stumbling blocks. She grew up in a Sephardic Jewish family under Benito Mussolini's fascist regime, after all. When her conservative father refused to let Rita or her sister pursue a formal education, she convinced him otherwise and graduated at the top of her class from medical school. Soon after, the Italian government's 1938 anti-Jewish Racial Laws forced her out of working in her university histology clinic. So Rita built a makeshift laboratory in her parents' house to continue experimenting. When her family was then forced to flee to a remote village to escape Nazi forces, Rita yet again refused to give up. She talked local farmers into giving her fertilized eggs, a key component in her experiments, by telling them her children needed the increased nutrition. Rita didn't even *have* children!

Rita's family survived World War II after going into hiding with a Catholic family in Florence. Once the war was officially over, she set her mind to the exhausting, grueling work of serving as a physician in an Allied displaced persons camp. But research was her calling, and Rita eventually moved to Missouri to study histology at Washington University in St. Louis.

When Rita arrived in the United States, her colleagues recommended she drop the name Levi in favor of Montalcini, since it was less recognizably Jewish. But Rita refused to hide her Jewish identity, and she combined both names professionally. Rita went on to discover an essential facet of nerve cell development called the nerve growth factor (NGF), a discovery seeded by her at-home labs during the war. It was so monumental, in fact, that she and her colleague, Stan Cohen, won the Nobel Prize in Medicine in 1986! Her work has helped chart new potential treatments for cancer, multiple sclerosis, schizophrenia, and more.

Rita used the obstacles she was forced to scale in her own life as fuel for social justice. Whether leading groundbreaking institutes or creating her own foundations, she spent the rest of her career providing other scientists with the support they needed in their own work. Rita did not stop researching or advocating for social justice until her death at age one hundred three.

JEWISH NOBEL-PRIZE LAUREATES

Jews have won the Nobel prize in all six categories: Physics, Chemistry, Physiology or Medicine, Literature, Peace, and Economic Sciences. These Jewish Nobel laureates hail from all over the world, including Germany, Argentina, Switzerland, South Africa, the Netherlands, Israel, and more!

Jewish looks like...
embracing chutzpah
in the face of obstacles.

BUREAU OF
CONTRACEPTIVE ADVICE

Bessie Moses

DOCTOR, PUBLIC HEALTH ADVOCATE | 1893–1965 | BALTIMORE, MARYLAND

BORN TO a German Jewish family in Baltimore, Maryland, in 1893, Bessie Moses's beliefs about women's rights were undoubtedly ahead of her time. Bessie had big dreams of becoming a doctor despite how difficult it was for women to pursue higher education. Her father was worried she wouldn't be able to find a suitable job, and encouraged her to become a teacher, just like her sister, instead. For two years, Bessie taught science to appease her father, but she was never satisfied. After convincing her family that her true path was in medicine, Bessie quickly returned to her studies, where she focused on women's health issues.

Dr. Bessie Moses achieved her childhood dream in 1922 when she graduated from Johns Hopkins University School of Medicine. At the time, there were fewer than twenty-five female doctors in all of Baltimore! Regardless of the many obstacles, Bessie was set on achieving her next big aspiration of opening a clinic that focused on contraceptives and women's health.

There was one seemingly unavoidable problem, though: no hospital would agree to house her clinic. That's because birth control was illegal and wouldn't become legal until decades later in 1965. Instead of giving up, Bessie got creative. She launched her clinic as a research facility called the Baltimore Bureau for Contraceptive Advice in a row house near the university in 1927. Not only was this Baltimore's first birth control clinic, but also one of the first to train both White and Black doctors on contraception and gynecological medicine.

Bessie's clinic eventually became the Baltimore Birth Control Clinic and then, ten years later, it became part of the Planned Parenthood Federation of America. In 1950, she and nurse Margaret Sanger were the joint winners of the Lasker Foundation Award in Planned Parenthood, the first women to ever win the honor! Bessie is a pioneering foremother to a long line of Jewish reproductive rights activists, including Betty Friedan, Gloria Steinem, and Heather Booth, the founder of the Jane Collective.

ABORTION RIGHTS AS A JEWISH VALUE

In the Talmud, ancient rabbis viewed the fetus as part of the mother, meaning that while pregnant, people are free to make their own choices about their bodies. Many Jewish leaders and organizations are at the forefront of reproductive justice to this day!

Jewish looks like... organizing for change.

Judith Heumann

DISABILITY RIGHTS ACTIVIST | DECEMBER 18, 1947–MARCH 4, 2023
PHILADELPHIA, PENNSYLVANIA

JUDITH HEUMANN proved time and time again that "disabled" does not mean "not able." Born to Jewish parents who escaped Nazi Germany, Judith and her brothers grew up in Brooklyn, New York. Judith contracted a disease called polio when she was eighteen months old and became a quadriplegic, needing a wheelchair to get around.

Judith and her family quickly found out that one of the big challenges disabled people face is dealing with other people's biases. When it was time for Judith to start kindergarten, the principal barred her from attending school. They claimed she was a fire hazard! Her mother tried to enroll her at a yeshiva, even making Judith learn Hebrew in order to meet the principal's requirements. But despite learning the language, Judith was still not allowed to attend.

Judith was finally admitted to school at nine years old, which was also the summer she went to camp for disabled kids. Camp was like being free for the first time ever! She and her new disabled friends had the space and trust to simply be themselves.

But this freedom seemed confined to her time at camp. When Judith grew up and applied to become a teacher, the Board of Education of the City of New York turned her down for a job. They assumed she couldn't teach simply because she couldn't walk. After winning her discrimination lawsuit, Judith proved just how wrong the board had been by teaching at the very same school she'd attended as a student. She was the first educator with a visible disability in the school's entire history.

Following her case, Judith and her friends founded a revolutionary group called Disabled in Action, which was run by and for people with disabilities. In 1977, after the US Secretary of Health, Education, and Welfare refused to sign regulations for Section 504 of the Rehabilitation Act of 1973, legislation that guarantees certain rights to people with disabilities, Judith led the longest nonviolent sit-in at a federal building in San Francisco. She and other disability activists protested for twenty-six straight days! The federal government did everything they could to stop them, including cutting off the water supply and phone lines in the building. But Judith pushed ahead, making sure that all disabled protestors were able to fully participate. In the end, their historical activism successfully forced the government to implement regulations. Even more far-reaching, Judith's leadership woke up the rest of the world to the importance of disability rights, an impact that's still reverberating to this day.

"Change never happens at the pace we think it should. It happens over years of people joining together, strategizing, sharing, and pulling

all the levers
they possibly can.
Gradually, excruciatingly
slowly, things start to
happen, and then suddenly,
seemingly out of the blue,
something will tip."

—JUDITH HEUMANN

Jewish looks like...
revering the
lifesaving
joy of discovery.

Baruj Benacerraf

IMMUNOLOGIST | OCTOBER 29, 1920–OCTOBER 2, 2011 | CARACAS, VENEZUELA

BARUJ BENACERRAF was born in Caracas, Venezuela, to a Moroccan Jewish father and Algerian Jewish mother and spent most of his childhood in Paris, France. This immersion in a range of cultures and experiences was ideal fodder for Baruj's unrelenting curiosity and joy of discovery. But the threat of World War II snuffed out his carefree childhood, and Baruj's family fled back to Venezuela.

As much as his father wanted him to take over the family textile business, Baruj's fascination with medicine was too consuming. He suffered from bronchial asthma as a child and was captivated by the invisible power of allergies. Why did certain substances cause his whole body to shut down, making it nearly impossible to breathe? And what could possibly be done about it? Baruj moved to New York to study science at Columbia University and graduated top of his class. He had the education, focus, and grades to pursue medical school at the highest level. But staunch antisemitism, including quotas limiting the number of Jewish students accepted, meant that Baruj was rejected from all twenty-five medical schools that he applied to. Thankfully, a concerned friend put in a good word, and Baruj was eventually accepted to the Medical College of Virginia.

Baruj's insatiable curiosity led him from allergies to the immune system, and he made one particular discovery almost by accident. Baruj happened to notice that guinea pigs that were genetically related to one another shared similar responses to antigens. It may sound obvious today that genes impact our immune system, but it was groundbreaking at the time! Baruj's work has influenced lifesaving medical breakthroughs around organ transplants, vaccinations, AIDS treatment, and more. He went on to win the Nobel Prize in Physiology in 1980, which is the same year he became president of the world-famous Dana-Farber Cancer Institute.

Against all odds, Baruj eventually held top teaching positions at the same medical programs that had rejected him as a student! It was in these universities where his passion for discovery extended beyond medicine to prioritizing learning from his students. In fact, Baruj is remembered as much for his generous, committed approach to his relationships as he is for his award-winning research.

IMMIGRATION OF JEWS TO LATIN AMERICA

Jews migrated to Latin America in waves throughout history. While Sephardic Jews first arrived in Latin America in the late 1400s as a means of escaping the Spanish Inquisition, some Moroccan Jews migrated to Peru and Brazil in the 1800s and became known as Amazonian Jews. The biggest wave of immigration occurred between 1880 and 1930 with Jews fleeing poverty, violent pogroms, and rising Nazism. Today, there are an estimated five hundred thousand Jewish Latin Americans spread all across the region!

Jewish looks like...
creating a hidden escape network that saved thousands of lives.

Doña Gracia Nasi

PHILANTHROPIST | 1510–1569 | LISBON, PORTUGAL

DOÑA GRACIA NASI was deeply devoted to her Jewish identity, even when it meant risking everything. Her ancestors fled from Spain most likely during the violent anti-Jewish Inquisition, only to be baptized into Catholicism once they arrived in Portugal. But like so many other conversos, or Jews forced to convert, Doña Gracia's family continued to practice Judaism behind closed doors. Their home was a safe haven to observe Shabbat, read sacred texts, and live proud Jewish lives. Even Doña Gracia's name was a secret! While she was officially born with the Catholic name Beatrice de Luna, her family called her by her Hebrew name in private: Gracia, or Hannah.

Doña Gracia married a fellow converso named Francisco Mendes, a successful merchant who traded all across Europe. After building an empire together for eight years, Mendes died and left his new widow with a young daughter . . . and one of the largest fortunes in Europe. Soon after, the Inquisition was reestablished in Portugal, and its target was secret Jews like Doña Gracia! She fled Portugal and continued chasing her full religious freedom everywhere from Belgium to Italy to Turkey.

After saving her own family, Doña Gracia Nasi used her resources and unrelenting bravery to develop a hidden escape network that saved thousands of other secret Jews! Doña Gracia took advantage of her extensive fleet of ships and business contacts to ferry runaway Jews across the Portuguese border. She then instructed her agents throughout Europe to help feed, clothe, and direct the refugees toward safe passage, which often included dangerous treks like crossing the Alps.

Doña Gracia continued to support her community by funding the translation of Hebrew Bibles into Spanish so that they could be more accessible to Sephardic Jews. Her charitable endeavors were unlike anything of her time, including funding rabbinic scholarship, hospitals, and synagogues across Europe. Doña Gracia Nasi died a beloved, celebrated hero who, in her final years, lived freely in Turkey as a Jew going by her cherished Hebrew name.

Doña Gracia Nasi and her husband may have held a grand wedding in a Catholic cathedral for the world to see . . . but they also held a private, secret Jewish ceremony where they signed their ketubah!

Jewish looks like...
leading with purpose.

Uri Ben Baruch

RELIGIOUS LEADER | 1898–DECEMBER 21, 1984 | BALNAGAB, ETHIOPIA | ISRAEL

URI BEN BARUCH didn't set out to be a leader. In fact, at first, he did his best to avoid it! He was born in the northern Ethiopian village of Balnagab in the Jewish community called Beta Israel. Uri studied under his father and other religious leaders and became known throughout the community for his knowledge and dedication. When it was time for the Beta Israel to receive a successor, many expressed their wish for Uri to be the one to lead them. He turned them down at first—he wasn't the oldest son and wanted to honor this sacred tradition. But after persistent encouragement from his community, he eventually accepted the role.

For centuries, the Beta Israel was separated from other Jewish communities and faced persecution within their larger Christian country. In 1966, Uri helped establish an organization called Beta Israel's Congregation, which had the goal of helping the Ethiopian Jewish community immigrate to Israel in order to preserve their future. For years, he wrote to Israeli leaders describing the challenges his people faced from both missions and government discrimination. They needed help and fast. His communications raised alarms for the Ethiopian Emperor, and Uri and his son were briefly arrested under suspicion of anti-government activities.

But in 1973, Uri Ben Baruch's letters and prayers were finally answered! The new chief rabbi of Israel, Rabbi Ovadia Yosef, received one of Uri's letters and immediately declared the Beta Israel part of the Jewish community. Under the Law of Return, which grants Israeli citizenship to any Jewish person around the world, the Ethiopian Jews were now able to move to Israel.

Many leaders do not live to see the fruits of their labor. However, up until his death in 1984, Uri Ben Baruch witnessed the immigration of tens of thousands of Ethiopian Jews to safety. All because of Uri's relentless belief in his people and the power of his pen!

ETHIOPIAN JEWS IN ISRAEL

Anti-Blackness is a universal issue that exists everywhere in the world, including Israel. While Israel is composed of Jewish people of all identities, colorism and racism are still a significant problem. Nearly the entire Ethiopian Jewish population lives in Israel; many of them face discriminatory attitudes there and are made to feel as if they are not Jewish enough. Belaynesh Zevadia was appointed as the country's first Ethiopian-born ambassador to Ethiopia in 2012.

Jews in the Community!

KESHET

Keshet works to ensure the full equality of all LGBTQ+ Jews and families. They equip Jewish organizations with the skills and knowledge to build LGBTQ+-affirming communities, create spaces in which all queer Jewish youth feel seen and valued, and advance LGBTQ+ rights nationwide.

"Jewish looks like . . . sweetness, struggle, and survival with joy in our hearts and a commitment to justice deep in our souls."

Idit Klein,
President and CEO of Keshet

Jewish looks like...
fighting for immigrant rights.

Give me your tired, your poor,
Your huddled masses yearning to breathe free,
The wretched refuse of your teeming shore.
Send these, the homeless, tempest-tost to me,
I lift my lamp beside the golden door!
—from "The New Colossus"

Emma Lazarus

POET, ACTIVIST | JULY 22, 1849–NOVEMBER 19, 1887 | NEW YORK, NEW YORK

WHEN EMMA LAZARUS'S Portuguese ancestors faced the violent horrors of the Inquisition, they left everything they knew in search of safety and hope. They became some of the very first Jewish immigrants to ever arrive in what would later become the United States! Approximately three hundred years after the Inquisition began in Portugal, Emma continued her ancestors' legacy by pursuing her own passionate fight for immigrant rights.

Emma and her seven siblings grew up in a loving family with access to significant opportunity. Emma had private tutors! Learned multiple languages! She even published a book of poems . . . as a teenager! Emma was a fiercely independent creative who crafted highly acclaimed poetry and prose.

But hers was not at all a common immigration story. In the 1880s, thousands of Ashkenazi Jews fled Russia's bloody pogroms. Just like Emma's own family centuries before, these refugees were fleeing anti-Jewish persecution in pursuit of a new beginning on America's shores. Yet, unlike Emma, they often faced hostile, destitute conditions.

Emma refused to passively stand by. She volunteered across New York City in support of refugees by teaching English, raising money, and even helping to establish the Hebrew Technical Institute to provide vocational training. Most important, she sat down with immigrants and listened to their stories. Emma then used her platform and resources to amplify the brutal injustice of their current conditions. She became an outspoken voice for Jewish rights, which was reflected in both her writing and activism.

Emma eventually poured her vision for immigrant rights and dignity into a sonnet called "The New Colossus." The poem helped raise money to build and erect the platform required for the Statue of Liberty to stand tall in New York Harbor. Years after her own death, Emma's words were engraved on the pedestal itself. They remain a rallying cry for hopeful Americans and immigrant rights activists to this day.

JEWISH POETRY

Jews have a rich history of literature and poetry spanning back to ancient times. Many songs or chants found in the Torah present themselves as poetry full of literary devices, such as metaphor and repetition. In the tenth century, Hebrew poetry extended beyond religious themes, and it flourished, particularly in Spain! This secular writing was a vehicle for Jews to express their ideas regarding society, culture, and government, all forms of literary activism that continue today.

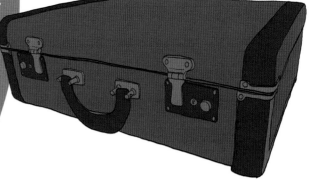

75

Abby Chava Stein

TRANSGENDER ACTIVIST, AUTHOR, RABBI, SPEAKER | b. OCTOBER 1, 1991
BROOKLYN, NEW YORK

ONE COULD SAY that Abby Chava Stein was destined to be a Jewish role model. After all, she is a living descendent of the Baal Shem Tov, the founder of Hasidic Judaism. But Abby's status as a leader within the Jewish community came in a form she never expected.

Growing up in Brooklyn as one of thirteen siblings, Abby was immersed in the Hasidic community. Her first language was Yiddish, followed by Hebrew and Aramaic, and she only came to learn English in her twenties. While Abby's upbringing is shared by many Hasidic Jews, her story took a different turn. Although she was assigned male at birth, Abby knew deep down that she was a woman of trans experience.

While searching for answers as a teenager, Abby drew comfort from the gender-fluid ideas of the Talmud, which recognizes six genders, as well as the Kabbalah, which says a man may be reincarnated into the body of a woman. But she knew there was a big difference between what the Talmud says and being openly accepted by her community. This painful tension contributed to Abby's battle with depression. Eventually, despite her rabbi prohibiting the internet, Abby began researching transgender identity online and finally felt affirmed. In order to live authentically as herself, she ultimately made the decision to leave the Hasidic community and begin her gender transition.

Today, Abby has redefined her identity in both her gender and her Judaism. She has proudly returned to her Jewish roots on her own terms, finding a new community within the Jewish Renewal movement, which centers mysticism, music, and spirituality. She has traveled the world, giving hundreds of speeches on issues related to the LGBTQ+ community, Judaism, antisemitism, and more. Abby is breaking ground as a bestselling author, rabbi, and activist, and she does it all while recognized by her true name. Her journey is a bright reminder that even in the oldest of communities, there is always space for change.

Abby was ordained as an Orthodox rabbi by the age of twenty.

Jazz Jennings

ACTIVIST, AUTHOR, REALITY STAR, SPOKESPERSON | b. OCTOBER 6, 2000 | FLORIDA

JAZZ JENNINGS grew up just like many of the girls in her neighborhood. She loved ballet, pretending to be a mermaid, and singing Broadway tunes at the top of her lungs. One difference? Jazz was assigned male at birth. With her family's support, Jazz proudly came out as a girl when she turned five years old.

Just one year later, in 2007, Jazz shared her story with Barbara Walters on the prime time television show *20/20*. Up until that moment, there was hardly any media visibility for transgender kids, and the stories that did exist usually centered on trauma and pain. But Jazz changed the game by taking up space and staying true to herself. She spoke proudly and joyfully about her identity with unequivocal support from her family. People from around the world—from President Barack Obama to Laverne Cox—have since celebrated Jazz's interview as a historic and groundbreaking moment for transgender visibility.

TRANSGENDER RIGHTS IN THE JEWISH COMMUNITY

In 2015, the Union for Reform Judaism officially adopted a transgender rights policy. While there is far more work to be done, Jews have historically fought at the forefront of LGBTQ+ activism and inclusion.

Unfortunately, not everyone was so supportive. In elementary school, Jazz was banned from competing on the girls soccer team. She felt humiliated, but it also emboldened her to take action. Instead of switching to the boys team or giving up soccer altogether, eight-year-old Jazz continued to practice with the girls. Jazz went on to work with the National Center for Lesbian Rights to challenge the US Soccer Federation's harmful ban and to create more inclusive policies . . . and they won!

Now, Jazz uses her voice to spread the values of love and acceptance in the fight for equal rights. Some of the countless other roles Jazz takes on include being a reality show star, YouTube content creator, and beauty spokesmodel, not to mention a children's book author. Yet more and more books centering LGBTQ+ and characters of color continue to be unjustifiably banned from schools and libraries. As a result, Jazz's award-winning picture book, *I Am Jazz*, has become one of the most banned books in the country. Just like every other time she's faced injustice in her life, Jazz uses her platform to speak out against censorship and advocate for change. Anything is possible for Jazz Jennings, the young woman who opened doors by remaining unwavering in who she has always been.

JEWISH CULINARY ARTS

When many people think about Jewish food, matzah balls and latkes immediately come to mind.

However, there's an entire world of Jewish cooking out there!

While Jewish cooking may have originated with the cuisine of the ancient Israelites, it has since expanded to include food from across the diaspora. Consider the foods Jews eat during Hanukkah! While Jews with ties to Eastern Europe eat potato latkes, Moroccan Jews eat Sfenj, Iraqi Jews eat soft Halva and Puerto Rican Jews eat spicy corvina ceviche. Creators from across the globe are putting Jewish food on the map, including chef Pati Jinich, who blends Mexican and Jewish delicacies, and food writer Benedetta Jasmine Guetta, who shares her Jewish and Italian culinary background on her popular blog!

Jewish looks like...
cooking up
Koshersoul.

Michael Twitty

AUTHOR, CULINARY HISTORIAN, EDUCATOR, CHEF | b. 1977 | WASHINGTON, D.C.

MICHAEL WAS BORN in Washington, DC, with a love for food and cooking. The flavors! The textures! The stories! Even though Michael was born into a Christian family, his mother would buy challah for Sunday supper on her way home from church and smother it with berry jams and apple butter. Later, when Michael turned seven years old, his mother taught him how to braid challah in their kitchen. It was in those moments together, fingers twisting dough into perfect loaves, that Michael first felt his Jewishness deep within his soul.

Michael's Jewish identity continued to grow alongside his love of cooking, and he was set on pushing against limiting boundaries in both areas of his life. As a young adult he found community in a Sephardic synagogue and eventually converted to Judaism when he was twenty-five years old. Knowing there was no existing word to reflect the richness of his roots, he created his own: Afro-ashke-phardi, a label combining his African, Ashkenazi, and Sephardic identities. Michael worked as a Hebrew school teacher while exploring the intricacies and intersections of food and culture. As a Black, gay, Jewish man, Michael sees food as a key that unlocks the truth about our history and ourselves—the painful parts, the beautiful parts, and everything in between. Michael's work confronts this tension head-on. He founded the Southern Discomfort Tour, which, by journeying through places that were important to his own ancestors during their enslavement, explores how racism influenced Southern cooking.

Michael continues to push boundaries as an award-winning chef, author, historian, and scholar, and he keeps Judaism and African American culture firmly at the center of his work. His award-winning cookbooks are in kitchens across the country, and his memoir *Koshersoul* won the 2022 National Jewish Book Award for Jewish Book of the Year. To Michael, hospitality and cooking is a mitzvah that offers a pathway to healing. He blends Jewish and Black cultures and histories from around the world into one delicious bite!

In his words, being Koshersoul is about "melding the histories, tastes, flavors, and diasporic wisdom of being Black and being Jewish."

Jewish looks like... claiming your identity while fighting for others.

Qian Julie Wang

CIVIL RIGHTS LAWYER, AUTHOR | b. JULY 24, 1987
SHIJIAZHUANG, CHINA | BROOKLYN, NEW YORK

MANY PEOPLE think of childhood as the most carefree time in their lives, but not Qian Julie Wang. She spent her early years in Shijiazhuang, China, doing things most kids love to do, especially dancing and playing in the sandbox. But right after Qian Julie's seventh birthday, her whole life was turned upside down: Qian Julie's family moved all the way to New York City.

Not only did Qian Julie find herself smack-dab in the middle of a brand-new country where she didn't understand the language, her family was also undocumented. Back in China, both of Qian Julie's parents worked as professors. But as undocumented immigrants in New York City, they could not get academic jobs. Instead, her parents worked long and difficult hours in labor-intensive sweatshops, living each day afraid of being discovered and sent back to China. Even in the hardest times, Qian Julie found comfort and belonging by going to the public library. Within those walls, she practiced English by reading books—*The Diary of Anne Frank* being one of her most beloved—and fell in love with classic characters, especially the Berenstain Bears.

Twenty-two years after setting foot in the United States, Qian Julie Wang was finally able to become an American citizen. Even though many of her worries were over, she never stopped wanting to help people just like her. She became a successful civil rights lawyer and tirelessly advocates for communities that have been marginalized. In 2020, Qian Julie represented a disabled child from a low-income immigrant family and fought for her educational rights. The success of this case will now help other children and families who find themselves faced with barriers that resulted from COVID-19, disability, and poverty. One year later Qian Julie published her memoir, *Beautiful Country*, which tells her story of growing up undocumented. It became a nationwide bestseller—even President Obama said it was one of his favorite books of the year!

After reading stories about Jewish values and perseverance, Qian Julie realized just how much Judaism resonated with her and converted as an adult. Now she speaks for justice everywhere she goes, including synagogues. In New York City, she helps create space for fellow Jews of color by blending her passion for racial and immigration justice with Jewish principles such as tikkun olam. Through her writing and activism, Qian Julie reminds us that fighting for justice is not an option for Jews: it's part of who we are.

JEWISH COMMUNITY IN CHINA

While many people do not think about China as a hub of Jewish history, there have been Jewish communities throughout the country for thousands of years! The Jews of Kaifeng in central China were established around 900 CE, and in the early 1900s there was a thriving Jewish population in the northern city of Harbin. Additionally, Shanghai became a haven for European Jews fleeing the Holocaust during World War II.

Jewish looks like...

mixing cultures
with delicious results.

Claudia Roden

CHEF, COOKBOOK AUTHOR, CULTURAL ANTHROPOLOGIST | b. 1936
CAIRO, EGYPT | LONDON, ENGLAND

NOTHING MAKES CLAUDIA RODEN happier than decadent smells wafting out of a bubbling pot, the tingle of spices on her tongue! Because for Claudia, cooking is more than a collection of ingredients: cooking is another way of building connections.

Born in Cairo to a Syrian Jewish family with Spanish roots, Claudia was destined to help open up the richness of Sephardic and Mizrahi cooking to the rest of the world. Claudia was surrounded by a myriad of cultures throughout her childhood. After all, her neighbors were Egyptian, Jewish, Spanish, Arab, Greek, Turkish, and Armenian! She would hear a tangle of beautiful languages spoken as she walked down the street, and she herself could join in on conversations in French, Italian, English, and Arabic. She even learned Ladino, the treasured language of Spanish Jews, from her grandmother.

In 1951, Claudia set off for boarding school in Paris, but little did she know that it would be thirty years before she would return to Egypt. A few years after her departure, Egypt was at war and Egyptian President Gamal Abdel Nasser expelled Jews and foreigners. Over twenty-five thousand Jews were forced to leave Egypt, including Claudia's family. They immigrated to London where Claudia now lives, never to return to Egypt again.

Claudia built community overseas just as she always had—by asking people about the foods their families ate together. What were their favorite dishes? What made *their* tongues tingle? While some people guarded their family recipes, Claudia saw exchanging recipes as a way of preserving cultural memory. Her family often hosted dinners for friends and family who also put down new roots in London, remembering the past and creating new beginnings together over heirloom family dishes.

Claudia strived to challenge stereotypes about food from Western Asia and North Africa, and knew the best way to bring others along was through their stomachs. So she turned her passion into the ultimate embodiment of her days of recipe swapping: writing cookbooks! In her first cookbook, *A Book of Middle Eastern Food*, Claudia introduced Westerners to new food and spice combinations. One of her most popular recipes is a delicious orange and almond cake, which pays tribute to the popularization of citrus harvesting by Sephardic Jews. In 1997, she won the National Jewish Book Award in the Sephardic and Ashkenazic Culture and Customs category for *The Book of Jewish Food*, and a lifetime achievement award at the sixteenth Jerusalem Jewish Film Festival for her contribution to culinary culture. Whether stirring a bubbling pot in Egypt or hosting a neighborhood Shabbat dinner in London, Claudia continues to spend her life bringing people together over the transformational power of food.

> Claudia's paternal great-grandfather was the chief rabbi of Aleppo, Syria.

Jews in the Community!
TEMPLE EMANU-EL OF DALLAS

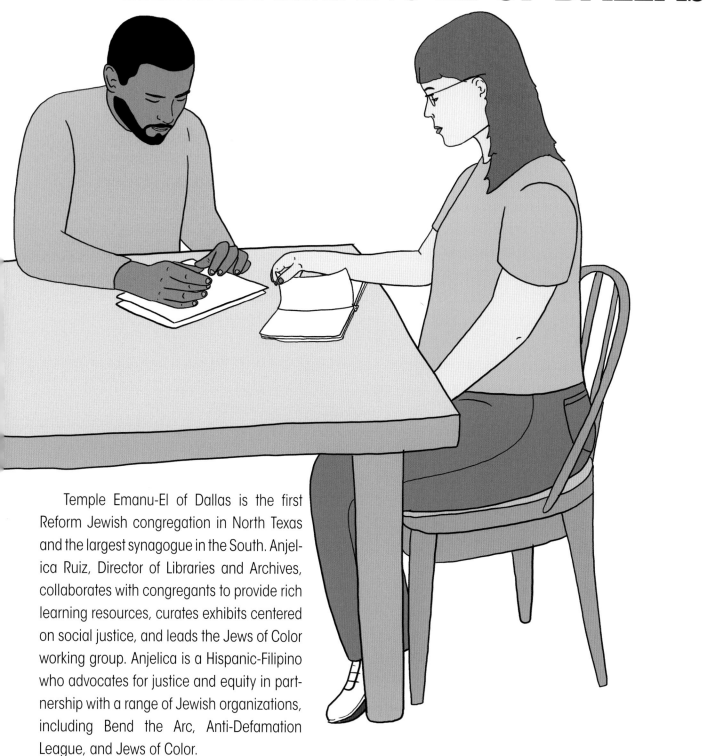

Temple Emanu-El of Dallas is the first Reform Jewish congregation in North Texas and the largest synagogue in the South. Anjelica Ruiz, Director of Libraries and Archives, collaborates with congregants to provide rich learning resources, curates exhibits centered on social justice, and leads the Jews of Color working group. Anjelica is a Hispanic-Filipino who advocates for justice and equity in partnership with a range of Jewish organizations, including Bend the Arc, Anti-Defamation League, and Jews of Color.

"*Jewish looks like...*
bringing all parts of ourselves to
the table. Our intersecting identities
only add to the rich tapestry
of the Jewish experience and
strengthens our community."

Anjelica Ruiz,
Director of Libraries and Archives, Temple Emanu-El of Dallas

89

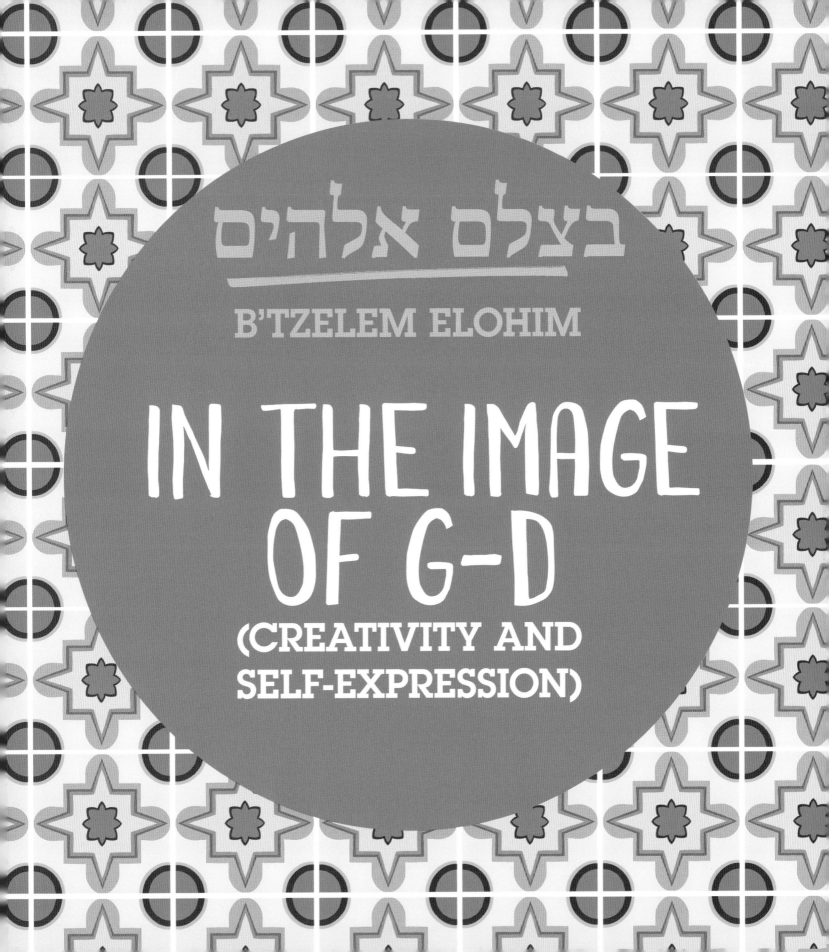

בצלם אלהים

B'TZELEM ELOHIM

IN THE IMAGE OF G-D

(CREATIVITY AND SELF-EXPRESSION)

Jewish looks like...
topping the charts
by staying
true to who
you are.

Ofra Haza

SINGER | NOVEMBER 19, 1957–FEBRUARY 23, 2000 | TEL AVIV-YAFO, ISRAEL

OFRA HAZA'S JEWISH PARENTS escaped religious persecution in Yemen and immigrated to Tel Aviv, where they raised nine children in the poor Hatikvah neighborhood. Ofra watched her mother perform songs beautifully for their community, particularly the traditional street music passed down from their ancestors. The Yemenite tin drums, mizmar, hand clapping . . . Ofra loved it all, especially singing!

Despite Ofra's own unmistakable talent, top composers and songwriters refused to take a chance on her mezzo-soprano voice. They were convinced that she was too Mizrahi for the mainstream music scene. But it was their loss. Ofra went on to release a number of hit records, including *The Prince of Egypt*'s famous song "Deliver Us"!

Ofra seemed to be at the top of her game, but she knew something was missing. She was constantly pushed into imitating her Western counterparts in both looks and music—Ofra's naturally frizzy hair was flat-ironed straight and her Mizrahi accent was minimized. In spite of her mainstream pop music's skyrocketing popularity, Ofra risked it all to return to her roots. She created a new wholly unexpected album full of the same Yemeni street songs she remembered from her childhood. Rather than stifle her blossoming career, her music took off even further! A breakout song from her album called "Im Nin'alu" was sampled by artists around the world, including Madonna. And the lyrics of that ever-popular song? A Mizrahi Jewish poem written by Shalom Shabazi, a beloved seventeenth-century Yemeni rabbi.

Ofra died unexpectedly at the age of forty-two due to complications from AIDS, but her legacy lives on today. By mixing traditional with contemporary and classic with pop sounds, Ofra Haza helped generate much deserved and long-awaited respect for Mizrahi music in Israel and around the world.

JEWISH BEAUTY STANDARDS

Ofra Haza was not the only Jewish woman who was told her appearance wasn't "European enough." For centuries, antisemitic tropes have circulated about Jewish people's physical features—especially mocking the idea that they have big noses and frizzy hair. Today, many Jews of all genders resist pressures to assimilate into Eurocentric beauty standards and, instead, embrace their features as a way of celebrating the authentic beauty of their own community.

Jewish looks like...
stepping into
the spotlight.

Ruby Myers

ACTRESS | 1907–OCTOBER 10, 1983 | PUNE, INDIA

RUBY MYERS was born in 1907 in Pune, India, to a Baghdadi Jewish family. This community of Jews began immigrating to India in the 1700s from Iraq. Other Jewish diasporas from around the Mediterranean immigrated as well, ultimately blending both Arabic and Indian cultures.

Ruby's talent as an actress sparkled in the Indian silent film industry, though she was most recognized by her chosen stage name: Sulochana. But Ruby did not grow up dreaming of stardom. How could she? Women were rarely seen in movies. They were expected to stay behind the scenes, not stand in the spotlight. Instead, Ruby worked for years as a telephone operator. That all changed the day a movie producer discovered Ruby and—despite her initial objections—convinced her to pursue acting. At first, Ruby had turned him down because of societal pressures regarding a woman's place, but she changed her mind when he offered her a leading role in his film! Ruby went on to star in popular silent films like *Wildcat of Bombay*, where she played not one but EIGHT different characters. Ruby was a full-blown superstar, eventually becoming the highest-paid female actor in all of India.

Ruby's ambition propelled her forward throughout her career. When talking films emerged, actors needed to be fluent in Hindustani. She didn't know a single word! Instead of giving up, she took a year off working to learn the language and went on to star in even more movies in the years to come. Ruby then took the bold, entrepreneurial steps of starting her very own production company, Rubi Pics, to create more opportunities within the industry. As time went on, Ruby struggled to land leading roles, and her career declined. Despite this, Ruby received the Dadasaheb Phalke Award, the highest award in India for lifetime achievement in film.

INDIAN JEWISH STARS

In the early years of the Indian movie industry, Hindu and Muslim women were often not allowed to perform on-screen. So Jewish women were cast in films instead. Ruby Myers wasn't alone in her stardom. Other groundbreaking Indian Jewish actresses included **Rose Musleah** (known as Miss Rose) and **Esther Victoria Abraham** (known as Pramila).

Sara Levi-Tanai

DANCER, CHOREOGRAPHER | c. 1910–OCTOBER 3, 2005 | ISRAEL

THE WORLD-RENOWNED, award-winning choreographer Sara Levi-Tanai overcame painful barriers to shine on the international stage. In the late 1800s, her parents traveled to their ancestral lands from Ethiopia, trekking over one thousand miles on foot. Sara was born in Jerusalem within a supportive community of fellow Yemenite Jews, but everything changed by the start of World War I. Her family was tragically forced into a refugee camp where everyone except Sara and her father died from typhus and starvation. As a means of surviving severe poverty, Sara's dad placed her in an orphanage.

Despite surviving on her own, Sara cultivated dreams of one day performing onstage. Sara carried these dreams with her as she and other girls were taken from the orphanage to a boarding school called Meir Shfeya, where she eventually became a nursery school teacher. Although Sara often lacked adequate teaching supplies, she was resourceful and wrote her own poem-based lessons that she set to music. These lyrical materials were packaged and shared with fellow teachers and are still used to educate generations of students to this day!

But Sara's greatest love was always theater and dance, a love that blossomed as she organized holiday pageants at the nearby kibbutz. Sara was committed to welcoming Yemenite Jewish immigrants who arrived during Operation Magic Carpet, making room at performances and inviting young people to train at the academy where she now worked. She felt deeply connected to their shared traditional songs and dances, far more than the European songs she was taught as a child in the orphanage. Sara was creatively electrified and soon founded a dance company that would become Inbal, which means "tongue of the bell" in Hebrew.

At Inbal, Sara invented an entirely new style and language of movement. Her dance company combined Yemenite and Jewish folklore to tell stories of her community's culture through music and motion. Sara went on to create over seventy ballets over the course of her career! Sara's passion for dance and her Yemeni heritage fuels a legacy of dance innovation that continues to influence choreographers around the world today.

YEMENITE JEWS AND OPERATION MAGIC CARPET

Jews have lived in Yemen for centuries, yet have continuously faced religious and ethnic persecution. In 1947, a pogrom claimed the lives of eighty-two Jews and destroyed numerous homes and Jewish businesses. This dangerous reality led to what became known as Operation Magic Carpet, which took place between June 1949 and September 1950, and saw the mass emigration of fifty thousand people—nearly the entire Yemenite Jewish community—to safety in Israel.

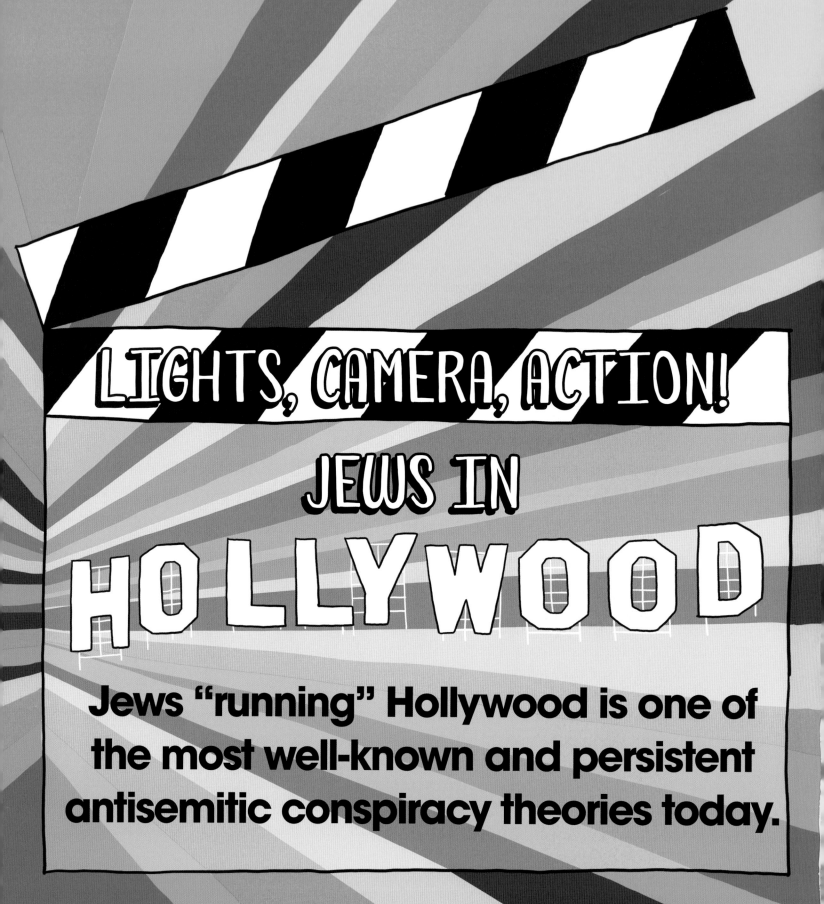

Jews do not, of course, control Hollywood

or the media at large. Like the garment business, film was one of the few industries that welcomed Jewish immigrants at the turn of the twentieth century. Aside from accessibility, it also tapped into a similar skill set that many Jewish people cultivated in their vibrant vaudeville neighborhood theaters! Many Protestant business owners and cultural elites frowned upon the "dirty" business of movies. But Jews channeled their entrepreneurial spirit into moviemaking, while also filling up theater seats alongside other immigrant communities. Jews have made great strides in the industry and, today, there is an even richer diversity of Jews behind and in front of the camera—from Taika Waititi to Abbi Jacobsen to Maya Rudolph!

Jewish looks like...
being "the only Black, Puerto Rican, one-eyed, Jewish entertainer in the world!"

Sammy Davis Jr.

ENTERTAINER | DECEMBER 8, 1925–MAY 16, 1990 | HARLEM, NEW YORK

SOME MIGHT SAY that Sammy Davis Jr. was destined to become a world-famous entertainer. His Afro-Cuban mother Elvera Sanchez was a chorus line dancer, and Sammy was trained in the art of performance by his African American father, Sammy Davis Sr., and godfather, Will Mastin. Born in Harlem in 1925, Sammy learned to do it all. Acting, singing, dancing, comedy, activism . . . there was no stopping the kid who would become one of the greatest entertainers of all time! Even as early as seven years old, Sammy starred as the lead in the Warner Brothers movie *Rufus Jones for President*!

Sammy rose to fame despite racist laws that discriminated against people who looked like him. He may have dazzled in Hollywood movies and been a member of the famous crew of entertainers called the Rat Pack, but Sammy was still forced to stay at "Black only" hotels when he was on the road. It didn't take long before he became an outspoken activist, performing at civil rights protests and joining Martin Luther King Jr. at the March on Washington in 1963.

Sammy eventually became friends with the Jewish comedian Eddie Cantor, who gave him a mezuzah as a gift. Even though mezuzahs are most often placed on the doorpost of Jewish homes, it meant so much to Sammy that he wore it around his neck for good luck! On the one night Sammy took it off, he lost his left eye in a terrible car accident. Sammy learned more and more about Judaism from the hospital's rabbi during his recovery. As a Black man, he described feeling emotionally tied to the suffering and strength of the Jewish people, and that he knew in his heart he needed to convert. Judaism developed into a critical piece of Sammy's identity, and Sammy became a bar mitzvah at forty-two. He even told the head of a major movie studio that he wouldn't work on Yom Kippur!

Until the end of his life, Sammy continued to break barriers as a singer, actor, cultural icon, and even photographer. It was Jerry Lewis, also known as the King of Comedy, who gave Sammy his first camera! Sammy's photos capture the ease that even the most world-famous celebrities felt in his presence and reveal a man whose artistic talent was boundless. A book of Sammy's own original photography was published seventeen years after he passed away.

CONVERTS

Some people are Jewish by birth, and others become Jews by converting. Both are equally Jewish! Sammy Davis Jr. converted to Judaism in the early 1960s. According to a 2014 Pew Research Study, 17 percent of American Jews were raised in another religion but became Jewish by choice.

Jewish looks like... **embodying irreverent creativity in all its forms.**

Taika Waititi

ACTOR, WRITER, DIRECTOR, PRODUCER | b. AUGUST 16, 1975
WAIHAU BAY, RAUKOKORE, NEW ZEALAND

WHAT IS TAIKA WAITITI'S answer to life's great questions? Creative expression, and a whole lot of it. Much of Taika's early years were a chaotic pull between living with his Jewish schoolteacher mother in Wellington, the busy capital of New Zealand, and with his native Te Whānau-ā-Apanui Māori artist father in the rural countryside. Despite the often-challenging tug-of-war of his childhood, Taika grounded himself through every form of creativity under the sun: painting, animation, photography, drama, stand-up comedy, and eventually filmmaking.

Creating art has always been how Taika makes sense of his various identities and place in the world. And not just any art—Taika's approach rips him from his comfort zone and pushes expectations around what is acceptable. Perhaps no movie better exemplifies Taika's creative risk-taking than his Academy Award–winning *JoJo Rabbit*, which is about a ten-year-old German boy who befriends a Jewish girl he discovers his mother is hiding in their attic during World War II. And who, exactly, does Taika play in this film? The child's buffoonish, imaginary best friend . . . Adolf Hitler. Taika uses this comedic portrayal to show the twisted seduction of fascist leaders, and how only compassion can overcome such hate. The story was inspired by not only his mother's family, who escaped pogroms in Russia, but also his Māori grandfather, who fought Nazis on behalf of New Zealand in the war.

The dynamic force that is Taika Waititi became the first Indigenous and Māori artist to ever win an Academy Award, and the hits haven't stopped there. He has since reimagined what is possible in blockbuster after blockbuster, including writing and directing movies for the Marvel universe.

Taika's pursuit of art is a celebration of joyful resilience and a commitment toward justice. He remains a steadfast advocate for marginalized communities in his professional work, including producing the award-winning show *Reservation Dogs*, which centers Indigenous teenagers in rural Oklahoma. His advocacy also extends into his activism, with Taika spearheading multiple anti-racism campaigns that have reached millions of people across New Zealand. Through his irreverent, innovative art and activism, Taika's lifelong commitment to creative expression continues to blaze trails and open minds.

> **"What better way to insult Hitler than having him portrayed by a Polynesian Jew?"**

Jewish looks like... returning home and sharing it with the world.

Ruth Behar

ANTHROPOLOGIST, POET, AUTHOR | b. NOVEMBER 12, 1956
HAVANA, CUBA | QUEENS, NEW YORK

RUTH BEHAR'S early childhood in Havana, Cuba, was filled with eating juicy pineapples, listening to batá drums, and strolling past the newly built Patronato synagogue. Her Ladino-speaking Turkish grandparents and Yiddish-speaking Polish and Russian grandparents found a welcoming home in Cuba after escaping persecution on the eve of the Holocaust. But as the Cuban Revolution came to an end in 1959, religious schools were shut down and atheism was imposed across the island. Five-year-old Ruth and her family joined the majority of the island's fifteen thousand Cuban Jews in fleeing their home. Eventually the family moved into a crowded apartment in Queens, New York.

Ruth longed for home back in Cuba. She struggled to learn English and was even penalized at school any time she spoke Spanish! At nine years old, Ruth's family was in a car crash that left her in a full body cast, unable to move for a full year. Ruth passed the days by turning to books, art, and—most of all—her imagination. She dreamed of traveling to faraway places, especially communities where she could speak Spanish again.

When Ruth finally went to college and discovered anthropology, the study of human societies and cultures, it was like her fantasies were magically coming true! She spent her career traveling to Spain, Mexico, and Cuba, exploring issues related to women and feminism. Ruth was ecstatic to return to her lost home and reconnect with her Cuban roots. This research fueled a stream of award-winning scholarship about Cuba's Sephardic Jewish community, including poetry, a documentary, an anthology, memoirs, children's books, ethnographic essays, and more. Her breakout middle grade novel *Lucky Broken Girl* won the 2018 Pura Belpré Award for most outstanding work of children's literature that honors the Latino cultural experience.

As the child of ancestors who fled genocide and were given safe refuge twice, Ruth understands the importance of welcoming immigrants with full compassion. She was named a Great Immigrant by the Carnegie Corporation and became the first Latino woman ever to win the MacArthur Genius Grant. Ruth Behar continues to center stories too easily forgotten and has made sense of her own understanding of home along the way.

THE JEWS OF CUBA

Cuba has been a home to Jewish immigrants fleeing persecution from around the world. The biggest wave came in the early 1900s when the United States limited immigration from eastern and southern Europe. Jews found refuge on the shores of Cuba and built synagogues, Yiddish theaters, radio stations, bakeries, and social clubs while still engaging deeply with Cuban culture.

Jews in the Community!
KAMOCHAH

"Jewish looks like . . .
a reflection of all the peoples and countries of the world."

—Maayan Zik, Cofounder of Kamochah

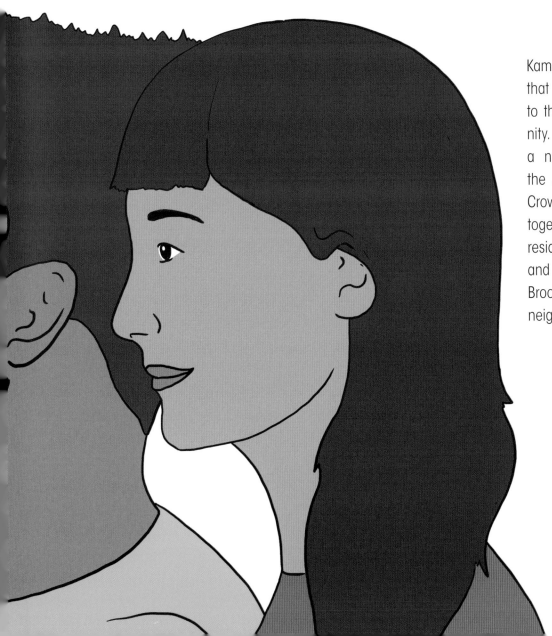

Kamochah is a nonprofit organization that exists to support and give a voice to the Black Orthodox Jewish community. Maayan also leads and organizes a number of other organizations in the Jewish community, including One Crown Heights, a coalition that brings together Black, Jewish, and Caribbean residents through advocacy, education, and activism to ensure Crown Heights, Brooklyn, is a safe, healthy, and thriving neighborhood.

More Jewish Folks
TO LEARN ABOUT!

AHUVA OZERI
March 3, 1948–
December 13, 2016
Israel
Singer, Songwriter, Composer

DOJA CAT
b. October 21, 1995
United States
Rapper, Singer, Songwriter

DRAKE
b. October 24, 1986
Canada
Rapper, Singer, Actor

ERIC ANDRÉ
b. April 4, 1983
United States
Comedian, Actor, Writer,
Producer, Musician

GLORIA SUZANNE KOENIGSBERGER HOROWITZ
b. November 21, 1951
Mexico
Astrophysicist

JAMIE MASADA
b. March 18, 1954
Iran
Businessman, Comedian

JUAN PABLO SORÍN
b. May 5, 1976
Argentina
Soccer Player

MASHALLAH IBN ATHARI
740 CE–815 CE
Iraq
Astrologer, Astronomer,
Mathematician

MAURICE SENDAK
June 10, 1928–May 8, 2012
United States
Children's Author, Artist,
and Illustrator

MAYA RUDOLPH
b. July 27, 1972
United States
Comedian, Actor, Writer,
Singer, Producer

P!NK
b. September 8, 1979
United States
Singer, Songwriter

RAFFI FREEDMAN-GURSPAN
b. May 3, 1987
Honduras; Activist
White House staffer

STEPHEN SONDHEIM
March 22, 1930–
November 26, 2021
United States
Composer and Lyricist,
Musical Theater Visionary

VOLODYMYR ZELENSKYY
b. January 25, 1978
Ukraine
Politician, President of
Ukraine

ZHAO YINGCHENG
1619–1657
China
Philosopher, Politician

Resources

LEARN MORE ABOUT WHAT JEWISH LOOKS LIKE

AVODAH: Supporting and developing Jewish social justice leaders https://avodah.net/racialjustice/

BE'CHOL LASHON: Strengthening Jewish identity by raising awareness around the ethnic, racial, and cultural diversity of Jewish identity and experience https://globaljews.org/

FACING HISTORY AND OURSELVES: Sharing educational resources and curriculum for educators to teach about standing up against antisemitism and other forms of hate www.facinghistory.org/

HEBCAL: Teaching about and keeping track of Jewish holidays happening all year long www.hebcal.com/

JEWS OF COLOR INITIATIVE: Providing research on perspectives and lived experiences of Jews of color https://jewsofcolorinitiative.org/research/

KESHET: Serving the LGBTQ+ Jewish community www.keshetonline.org/resources/topic/activism-and-allyship/

MY JEWISH LEARNING: Offering an online resource bank of articles, videos, and other resources to help navigate all aspects of Judaism and Jewish life www.myjewishlearning.com/

PJ LIBRARY: Sending free Jewish books to Jewish families and offering book lists and educational resources for kids and caregivers https://pjlibrary.org/home

RESPECTABILITY: Creating resources and guides to support Jews with disabilities and make Jewish spaces more inclusive www.respectability.org/jewish-toolkit/

Acknowledgments

WE'VE HIGHLIGHTED a number of Jewish values, but there's still one more we'd like to share: Hakarat hatov, which means showing gratitude, or literally "recognizing the good." This book is a labor of love from our entire beautiful community, those who inspired us, questioned us, spoke with us, and supported us throughout this endeavor.

To our talented illustrator, Iris, who brought this book to life; our agents Emily Sylvan Kim and Ginger Knowlton for being our relentless champions; our amazing editor Luana Kay Horry, who shared our vision and helped it become a reality, along with Erika DiPasquale and Nancy Inteli; our supportive publisher, Liate Stehlik; the visionaries Jenna Stempel-Lobell and Amy Ryan in design; Jai Berg, Mark Rifkin, Annabelle Sinoff, Nicole Moulaison, and the tireless production team; Kerry Moynagh and the fabulous team in sales; Robby Imfeld, Nellie Kurtzman, and the hard-working marketing team; and to all the other wonderful folks at HarperCollins for turning our dream into something we can hold in our hands: thank you from the bottom of our hearts.

To those who generously gave their time to share their experiences and expertise: Rabbi Danya Ruttenberg, Julian Voloj, Ilana Kaufman, Idit Klein, Maayan Zik, Anjelica Ruiz, and Rabbi David E. Stern, thank you for everything. We are overjoyed that your wisdom is encapsulated in this book for generations to come. To the creators who offered their gorgeous minds and support at different stages in the writing process: Liz Garton Scanlon, Carla Naumburg, Catriella Friedman, Jen Brabander, Pnina Saloman, Madelyn Travis, Susan Kusel, Nadia Forte, Chris Barash, Shoshana Greenwald, and Joanna Ho . . . thank you for sharing your light with us.

None of this would matter without community. I (Liz) first and foremost want to express my love and appreciation for my brilliant friend and writing partner, Caroline. I'm so glad you picked up my call that day and said yes to embarking on this journey together! To my incredible partner, Christian; my parents; and those in the beautiful Jewish community (both online and in person) who supported my own learning and have cheered for me along the way. I wouldn't have done this without y'all.

I (Caroline) am still in awe that Liz came into my life and trusted me to build this project alongside her. Your wisdom, humor, and sense of purpose animate everything you touch and serve as the heartbeat of this book. To my unwavering family, my dear friends, my beloved Tavita, and my deliciously curious and patient kiddos, Afi, Manu, Leone, and Tala: I can't thank you enough for learning alongside me and showing up in your own beautiful ways. I love you always, always!